Poverty

by Tina Kafka

LUCENT BOOKS

A part of Gale, Cengage Learning

Detroit • New York • San Francisco • New Haven, Conn • Waterville, Maine • London

LIBRARY OF CONGRESS CATALOGING-IN-PUBLICATION DATA

Kafka, Tina, 1950-
 Poverty / by Tina Kafka.
  p. cm. -- (Hot topics)
 Includes bibliographical references and index.
 ISBN 978-1-4205-0149-0 (hardcover)
 1. Poverty. 2. Globalization--Economic aspects. 3. Technological
innovations--Economic aspects. I. Title.
 HC79.P6K33 2010
 339.4'6--dc22

                                                         2010008075

Lucent Books
27500 Drake Rd.
Farmington Hills, MI 48331

ISBN-13: 978-1-4205-0149-0
ISBN-10: 1-4205-0149-6

Printed in the United States of America
1 2 3 4 5 6 7 14 13 12 11 10

Printed by Bang Printing, Brainerd, MN, 1st Ptg., 07/2010

CONTENTS

FOREWORD

Young people today are bombarded with information. Aside from traditional sources such as newspapers, television, and the radio, they are inundated with a nearly continuous stream of data from electronic media. They send and receive e-mails and instant messages, read and write online "blogs," participate in chat rooms and forums, and surf the Web for hours. This trend is likely to continue. As Patricia Senn Breivik, the former dean of university libraries at Wayne State University in Detroit, has stated, "Information overload will only increase in the future. By 2020, for example, the available body of information is expected to double every 73 days! How will these students find the information they need in this coming tidal wave of information?"

Ironically, this overabundance of information can actually impede efforts to understand complex issues. Whether the topic is abortion, the death penalty, gay rights, or obesity, the deluge of fact and opinion that floods the print and electronic media is overwhelming. The news media report the results of polls and studies that contradict one another. Cable news shows, talk radio programs, and newspaper editorials promote narrow viewpoints and omit facts that challenge their own political biases. The World Wide Web is an electronic minefield where legitimate scholars compete with the postings of ordinary citizens who may or may not be well-informed or capable of reasoned argument. At times, strongly worded testimonials and opinion pieces both in print and electronic media are presented as factual accounts.

Conflicting quotes and statistics can confuse even the most diligent researchers. A good example of this is the question of whether or not the death penalty deters crime. For instance, one study found that murders decreased by nearly one-third when the death penalty was reinstated in New York in 1995. Death penalty supporters cite this finding to support their argument that the existence of the death penalty deters criminals from committing murder. However, another study found that states without the death penalty have murder rates below the national average. This study is cited by opponents of capital punishment, who reject the claim that the death penalty deters murder. Students need context and clear, informed discussion if they are to think critically and make informed decisions.

The Hot Topics series is designed to help young people wade through the glut of fact, opinion, and rhetoric so that they can think critically about controversial issues. Only by reading and thinking critically will they be able to formulate a viewpoint that is not simply the parroted views of others. Each volume of the series focuses on one of today's most pressing social issues and provides a balanced overview of the topic. Carefully crafted narrative, fully documented primary and secondary source quotes, informative sidebars, and study questions all provide excellent starting points for research and discussion. Full-color photographs and charts enhance all volumes in the series. With its many useful features, the Hot Topics series is a valuable resource for young people struggling to understand the pressing issues of the modern era.

INTRODUCTION

THE CYCLE
OF POVERTY

Everyone agrees that poverty is a serious global problem, but opinions vary widely about how to define it, what to blame for its broad reach, and how to fix it. Poverty is not like a disease that can be cured with the right medicine. It is a web of causes and effects so entangled and fragile that one slight change causes the entire web to tremble.

This was demonstrated in the 2008–2009 financial crisis, which began in the United States. Millions of people experienced difficulty paying their mortgages. Housing prices plummeted. With homeowners unable to pay for their homes, the banks had less money available to loan to businesses. Unemployment rose to levels not seen in many years, causing many Americans to slip into poverty. At the same time, demand for energy increased worldwide, and food crops such as corn and soybeans were diverted to biofuel production. As demand for these crops increased, prices for some grains rose so much that farmers had a difficult time feeding their livestock. Some farmers could not even pay for the very grain they harvested. Their families faced the threat of going hungry. World hunger, always a problem, became even more severe.

Poverty has its own momentum, which is often called "the cycle of poverty." Once the cycle of poverty begins to roll, it is hard to stop. As people lose their income, they often lose their shelter and access to food and clean water. Their health suffers;

diseases spread, yet access to health care may be limited. Without secure housing and good health, children find it difficult to attend school regularly. Without a good education, overcoming poverty becomes even more challenging. Thus, the cycle of poverty often extends from one generation to the next. If a child is born into a family living in poverty, he or she is more likely to remain in poverty for life than a child who is not born into poverty.

Many governments and organizations around the world, including the United Nations (UN), the World Bank, and nonprofit organizations—often called nongovernmental organizations, or NGOs—devote resources to finding solutions to poverty. But even as efforts increase, the problems multiply. In June 2009 the UN's World Food Program reported that there were more than one billion hungry people around the world. Josette Sheeran, the food program's executive director, told a British news agency that the world faced a human catastrophe as more people struggle to eat a decent meal. She reported, "This year we are clocking an average of four million new hungry people a week, urgently hungry."[1] That represented an increase of 105 million hungry people in the first six months of 2009.

It is common to hear people say that the world is shrinking. The expression does not refer to its physical size, of course. The world is shrinking because countries are more dependent on each other and less isolated from each other than they were in past times. At the dawn of the twenty-first century, communication technology and the Internet have lessened the isolation of even the most remote cultures and communities.

Technology may turn out to be the fabric that helps to strengthen the interconnections between people worldwide. In a world connected by technology, awareness of global poverty issues will likely increase, and each human resident of the planet will have a greater understanding of the issues that contribute to poverty. Understanding promotes action. Some people have more power than others to contribute to the solutions. But greater understanding guides all people to take whatever steps they can in the right direction.

Opinions differ widely about which issues should be tackled first and how they should be approached. Nonetheless, most people agree that poverty's consequences are widespread and devastating. Fortunes depend on whether or not the world community musters its forces to narrow the vast divide between those who have and those who have not.

FINDING THE POVERTY LINE

There is no simple way to define poverty. But poverty experts must be able to work together and understand each other when they discuss, analyze, and formulate plans to battle this common enemy. These experts have come up with some terms that help define the lines between who is poor and who is not. Categorizing countries that share common features associated with poverty may also be useful. Even so, the lines and categories of poverty are never clear cut, and experts disagree over which terms and categories are best. Experts juggle these terms as they strive to reach understandings that will help them work together to lift people out of poverty.

The Line No One Wants to Cross

The poverty line, or poverty threshold, is usually defined as the minimum level of income necessary to maintain a decent standard of living, either within one country or region or worldwide. Poverty lines themselves are adjusted periodically to account for changes in the cost of living. For example, until 2008, the World Bank, an institution that provides financial assistance to the poorest countries, set the poverty line at $1 a day for people living in the poorest countries. In effect, people who lived on $1 or less were considered to be living in extreme poverty. That figure, however, was based on prices for goods and services in 1993. In 2004, using that measure, 985 million people worldwide lived below the poverty line. Then in 2008, the World Bank raised the international poverty line to $1.25. The change reflected updated costs of living. As surprising as it may seem, that twenty-five-cent increase plunged 430 million more people below the new poverty line.

There are different ways to determine poverty lines. This is important because the way poverty is measured changes the way governments and organizations handle their antipoverty programs. Douglas Besharov of the American Enterprise Institute explained in a 2001 interview how changing the poverty line affects poverty programs in the United States. After the 2000 United States Census, experts disagreed about whether to raise the poverty line to reflect changing incomes and prices. According to Besharov, "There is a political battle, a minor skirmish going on here with a number of people favoring the new measure because it would raise the count of poor and thus the need for more programs and more spending."[2] In the United States, being able to collect benefits such as food stamps, welfare, and children's health care depends on which side of the poverty line people fall.

Absolute Poverty

Poverty is generally discussed in terms of *absolute* poverty and *relative* poverty. Absolute measures of poverty determine a poverty line or threshold and then simply count the number of people who fall below that line. Measures of absolute poverty consider basic products and services that people need to live. They include food, shelter, clean water, sanitation, and access to basic health care and education. The assumption behind measures of absolute poverty is that regardless of where people live, their basic needs are essentially the same.

There are benefits to measuring poverty in this way. Absolute poverty measures apply the same standards across cultures, geographic locations, and time periods. Therefore absolute measures enable experts to compare standards of living around the world and over time. However, absolute measures do not account for the reality that resources, needs, and costs are not the same everywhere. People who live in cold climates require a source of heat during the winter, whereas people on tropical islands do not. Heat requires energy. Energy costs money.

To try to address these issues, David Gordon, a professor of social justice at the University of Bristol in England, prepared a report for the United Nations in 2005 to help clarify absolute

People without access to nearby water who also live in a shelter with a mud or dirt floor are considered to be living in absolute poverty.

poverty. Gordon suggests that absolute poverty is the absence of any two of eight basic needs: adequate food, safe drinking water, sanitation facilities, health care, adequate shelter, access to information, and access to services (including education, health, legal, social, and financial). He also qualifies each basic need. For example, Gordon defines adequate shelter and safe drinking water in this way: "Homes must have fewer than four people living in each room. Floors must not be made of dirt, mud, or clay. Water must not come solely from rivers and ponds, and must be available nearby (less than 15 minutes' walk each way)."[3] According to Gordon's assessment, someone who never attended school and cannot read is considered severely deprived of education. If that person also lives in a home with mud floors, he or she is considered to be living in absolute poverty, since that person lacks two of the eight basic needs (adequate shelter and access to services). By qualifying and further defining basic needs, Gordon's definition accounts for the differences in the costs of those needs in various places.

Relative Poverty

Most experts agree, however, that measures of absolute poverty are insufficient. Not only do basic needs differ from place to place, but cultural expectations differ, too. To account for these differences, experts measure relative poverty, which compares people with each other. Relative poverty measures account for the social ties that people have to others. In the wealthiest countries, the poor may not live in absolute poverty. They may have access to the basic necessities, and may, in fact, live in relative comfort compared with those who live in poverty in other places.

POVERTY IS MORE THAN A LACK OF WEALTH

"Well-being isn't just about our relationship with things, it's also about our relationships with each other. Poverty hurts, not just because it can leave you feeling hungry, cold and sick, but because it can also leave you feeling ignored, excluded and ashamed."—Adam Smith, economist and philosopher

Quoted in Gavin Kennedy (blog), "Adam Smith on Poverty," Adam Smith's Lost Legacy, June 22, 2008. http://adamsmithslostlegacy.com/2008/06/adam-smith-on-poverty.html.

While relative poverty satisfies the need for different measures for different places, it also tends to highlight the inequality that exists between people who live in the same country. This is because measures of absolute poverty are objective. Someone either lives above or below the line. Relative poverty, on the other hand is subjective; it compares living standards. Someone may be poorer than someone else, but neither may live in absolute poverty. The consequences of inequality can be devastating. As the gap between the rich and poor widens, crime increases, health and education suffer, and families suffer. Anup Shah, whose Web site Global Issues addresses many of these issues, explains: "Some of these things are hard to measure, such as the level of trust

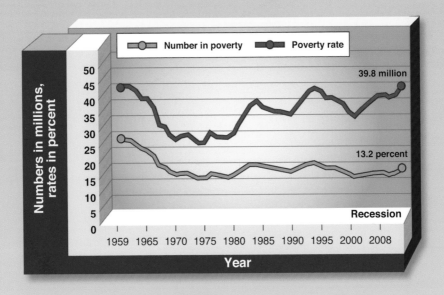

Number in Poverty and Poverty Rate: 1959 to 2008

Number in poverty • Poverty rate

Numbers in millions, rates in percent

50
45
40
35
30
25
20
15
10
5
0

39.8 million

13.2 percent

Recession

1959 1965 1970 1975 1980 1985 1990 1995 2000 2008

Year

Taken from: U.S. Census Bureau, Current Population Survey, 1960 to 2009 Annual Social and Economic Supplements.

and comfort people will have in interacting with one another in the society. Nonetheless, numerous studies report that the poor in wealthy countries can be unhappier or find it harder to cope than poor people in poorer countries."[4]

For example, almost every family in the United States owns at least one color television. Yet this appliance that sits in the living rooms and bedrooms of most U.S. homes is rare in parts of the world where electricity is absent or unreliable. Therefore a resident of the United States without a television might feel deprived, while someone in a less-developed country who lives in a region without electricity would not expect to own a television at all. Moreover, even the poorest families in the United States have ready access to clean water, which flows from taps and flushes toilets. Such easy access to clean water is unimaginable in many parts of the developing world.

The United Nations Defines Poverty

In the ongoing attempt to clarify the definition and causes of poverty, the heads of all agencies within the United Nations signed this statement in June 1998:

> Fundamentally, poverty is a denial of choices and opportunities, a violation of human dignity. It means lack of basic capacity to participate effectively in society. It means not having enough to feed and clothe a family, not having a school or clinic to go to, not having the land on which to grow one's food or a job to earn one's living, not having access to credit. It means insecurity, powerlessness and exclusion of individuals, households and communities. It means susceptibility to violence, and it often implies living on marginal or fragile environments, without access to clean water or sanitation.

UN Statement, June 1998, quoted in David Gordon, "Indicators of Poverty and Hunger," University of Bristol, December 12–14, 2005, p. 4. www.un.org/esa/socdev /unyin/documents/ydiDavidGordon_poverty.pdf.

Concept of Relative Poverty Relatively Old

Two hundred years ago, economist Adam Smith addressed the issue of inequality in his book *The Wealth of Nations*. He writes, "A linen shirt, for example, is, strictly speaking, not a necessary of life. The Greeks and Romans lived very comfortably though they had no linen. But the present time, through the greater part of Europe, a creditable day-laborer would be ashamed to appear in public without a linen shirt."[5] This example of inequality is widely cited by other economists and poverty experts to emphasize the issue of inequality. Smith is also credited with highlighting the association of poverty with shame. Most experts agree that this connection accounts for many of the social problems associated with poverty.

A Nobel Prize Winner's Theory

Amartya Sen, an Indian economist and Harvard professor, spends his professional life investigating the roots of the inequality of poverty. Sen grew up in India in the 1940s in the midst of a serious famine. Sen's family and the families of his friends led normal lives, but every day he witnessed starving people begging for food in the streets. In fact, 3 million Indians died of hunger during the Bengal famine in 1943. Though he was a young boy, Sen was disturbed and puzzled by the fact that in the same place, some people starved while others had enough to eat.

Seeking the reasons for this inequality became the focus of Sen's work, both as a student and later as an economics professor. His studies confirmed his early suspicion that famine, one serious consequence of poverty, usually affects only a small proportion of the population—usually no more than 5 percent. Moreover, the factor most responsible for who has food and who does not is not the availability of food, but the form of a country's government. Governments that do not elect leaders in democratic elections have little interest in protecting their most

Amartya Sen, an Indian economist and Harvard professor, grew up in India during a serious famine. Sen spends his life studying poverty, and won the Nobel Prize in Economics in 1998.

economically vulnerable citizens, Sen found. This finding held true in every country he studied, including China, the Soviet Union, and countries in sub-Saharan Africa.

When asked to explain, Sen says, "The first answer is that the government servants and the leaders are upper class. They never starve. They never suffer from famine, and therefore they don't have a personal incentive to stop it. However, if the government were vulnerable to public opinion, then famines are a dreadfully bad thing to have. You can't win many elections after a famine."[6] Sen points out that poverty and its effects are a complex combination of political, social, and economic factors. Sen's best-known book, *Poverty and Famines*, was published in 1981. He won the Nobel Prize for Economics in 1998 for his work on poverty and democracy. Decisions about foreign aid for developing countries are often based on Sen's work.

MONEY BUYS SECURITY FROM FINANCIAL PRESSURES

"Money can't buy happiness . . . but it can buy security. Without huge financial pressures, people are free to enjoy life without worrying how they will provide for themselves and their loved ones."—College Student

Quoted in David Leonhardt, Readers' Comments, "Maybe Money Does Buy Happiness After All," *New York Times*, April 16, 2008. http://community.nytimes.com/comments /www.nytimes.com/2008/04/16/business/16leonhardt.html.

Developing and Developed Countries

Regardless of whether poverty is discussed in absolute or relative terms, and despite the political issues involved, fighting poverty on a global scale requires cooperation. World governments, the United Nations, and other global institutions, as well as antipoverty agencies, must work together to battle this pervasive problem. The most powerful weapon in that arsenal is shared understanding. To that end, countries are generally divided into economic categories. These categories are based on several factors, which include the income of people who live there, the rate of literacy, and how efficiently a country runs its business and industry.

The world's poorest countries are generally referred to as "developing countries." In general, these countries have low rates of literacy; high rates of disease and malnutrition; lack of basic infrastructure such as roads, systems of communication, and energy; and poor living conditions. In many developing countries, powerful leaders make the major economic decisions and control the wealth. These leaders may not be interested in helping the poor. They may not have enough resources, or they may not know how to manage resources. People who live in developing countries may have little input into or influence with the government or economy of the place in which they live, so their needs are not a priority for the leaders or the government.

In developed countries such as the United States, the living standard is generally higher and all children must attend school.

Obama's Message to Ghana

United States president Barack Obama and his family visited Ghana in summer 2009 on his first official visit to a country in sub-Saharan Africa. Crowds lined the street in the capital city of Accra to greet the first African American U.S. president. Obama's father was born in the African country of Kenya, and Obama speaks of a special connection to the people of Africa. His message in Ghana was warm, but stern. He cautioned that Ghana must monitor the honesty of its institutions and government. He said, "No country is going to create wealth if its leaders exploit the economy to enrich themselves, or police can be bought off by drug traffickers. No business wants to invest in a place where the government skims 20 percent off the top, or the head of the port authority is corrupt. No person wants to live in a society where the rule of law gives way to the rule of brutality and bribery. That is not democracy; that is tyranny, and now is the time for it to end. Africa doesn't need strongmen. It needs strong institutions." Obama's emphasis on democracy is fitting in Ghana, since the former British colony became a functioning democracy in 1992. Its government is relatively stable in a continent that is marked by civil wars and conflict. Obama praised Ghanaian president John Atta-Mills for his focus on reducing corruption.

Quoted in Peter Baker, "Obama Delivers Call for Change to a Rapt Africa," *New York Times,* July 12, 2009, p. 10.

President Barack Obama and First Lady Michelle Obama shake hands with the people of Ghana at a hospital in Accra during his 2009 visit.

"Developed" countries such as the United States and most of western Europe lie at the opposite end of the spectrum. In developed countries, democratically elected representatives make most important decisions. These representatives have more motivation to serve the people who elect them, both rich and poor. Business and industry is privately owned. Industries in developed countries usually operate with modern technology. Prices for products and wages for workers in developed countries are determined by the market, not by the government or a strong leader. When products are plentiful, prices fall, and when supplies are limited, prices rise. By the same token, employment remains high when the economy is strong and falls if the economy weakens.

While wealthy countries have areas where housing is substandard and unemployment is high, the overall living standard is generally higher in developed countries than it is in developing countries. Almost everyone in the United States, for example, owns a phone, a television, and a car if they need to drive to work. They have food and access to a washer and dryer to clean their clothes. All U.S. children must attend school, and almost every adult citizen in the United States has the right to vote.

In a speech to the United Nations in 2000, Kofi Annan, then secretary general of the United Nations, distinguished between developed and developing countries. He said, "A developed country is one that allows all its citizens to enjoy a free and healthy life in a safe environment. And a genuinely developing country is one in which civil society is able to insist, not only on material well being, but on improving standards of human rights and environmental protection as well."[7] The United Nations has named forty-nine countries, including thirty-three in Africa, several in eastern Europe, and ten in Asia as "least developed." The United States, Canada, Japan, Australia, New Zealand, Israel, South Africa, and most countries in western Europe are generally considered developed nations by the world at large.

Many countries do not fall neatly into either the "developing" or the "developed" category. Some are undergoing rapid economic changes. These countries are said to be countries with "transitional economies." Many countries in eastern Europe that were once part of the Union of Soviet Socialist Republics (USSR), China, and Vietnam are among those countries that are in transition.

Poverty Around the World

Poverty has different causes in different parts of the world, but the effects of extreme poverty are universally devastating. A majority of the world's poorest countries are found in Africa, though some African countries are poorer than others. South Africa and Egypt, for example, fare better than Angola and Ethiopia. While absolute poverty has decreased in some African nations, the poverty in many African countries relative to the rest of the world has actually increased.

Poverty in Africa has multiple causes. In many parts of Africa, farmers rely solely on rainfall for irrigation. Food production, therefore, has been devastated by ongoing drought. Civil war in some African countries has created great economic hardship for many Africans; millions have been forced by war or other violent conflict to become refugees in neighboring countries. Others threatened by ethnic violence have lost their source of income. Lack of access to clean water in Africa results in the spread of diseases, which also complicates efforts to improve education and health care. AIDS is a pervasive and serious problem that wreaks havoc on many elements of African life.

Poverty in Latin America, like poverty in Africa, is widespread and more severe in some countries than others. The native peasants suffer most from poverty. In some regions, the land itself presents challenges. Rocky, mountainous terrain and climatic challenges such as extreme heat and cold make it difficult to transport products and build and maintain roads and energy plants. Millions of acres of rain forests in South and Central America are being cleared annually for short-term benefit, such as agriculture and products for wealthy countries, yet their destruction results in long-term devastation for peasant farmers who depend on rain forests for lifestyle and resources.

Southeast Asian countries like Cambodia continue to suffer extreme poverty with lack of education, unsafe housing, and hunger.

Population growth, migration, the drug trade and political instability also add to the ongoing poverty in Latin America. However, the news in Latin America is not all bad. While poverty is still serious in some countries, such as Peru, Ecuador, and Paraguay, it has improved in others, notably Mexico. One sign of improvement in Mexico is the rising number of children who stay in school beyond the primary grades.

Asia is home to the majority of the world's poorest people. In fact, Asia is home to the majority of the world's population overall. Though China has made remarkable progress in recent years, and the economies of Japan and South Korea are growing, widespread poverty persists throughout the continent. South Asia (including parts of India, Bangladesh, and Nepal) and Southeast Asia (including Cambodia, Laos, East Timor, and Myanmar) and even many regions in East Asia, including China's interior and North Korea, continue to suffer extreme poverty. Disease, lack of education, hunger, and unsafe housing—all consequences of extreme poverty—afflict the people in these regions just as they do the impoverished populations in Africa and Latin America and other parts of the world.

Poor in a Rich World

Yet, populations in poor countries are not alone in their struggles with poverty. People live in poverty in some of the richest countries as well. Wealth is rarely distributed equally. Some experts estimate that up to 25 percent of the population of the United States is relatively poor, while 2 to 3 percent live in absolute poverty. In the United Kingdom, national welfare policies limit absolute poverty, but some experts still consider up to 20 percent of the UK relatively poor. The poor in rich countries face just as many challenges as the poor in developing countries in overcoming their financial difficulties. In wealthy countries, the poor are often blamed for their financial difficulties, which makes it that much harder to find jobs and improve prospects. The cycle of poverty is difficult to stop anywhere in the world.

A study published in 2002 by leading world economist Branko Milanovic underscored the vast differences between the world's richest and poorest citizens. Milanovic studied ninety-one countries making up 85 percent of the world's population. He concluded that the richest 1 percent of people in the world earned as much as the poorest 57 percent put together. An article in a British newspaper highlighted the results of the study. It pointed out, "Four fifths of the world's population live below what countries in North America and Europe consider the poverty line. The poorest 10% of Americans are still better off than two-thirds of the world population."[8]

Other statistics are often quoted to highlight the wide gap between the world's rich and poor. Anup Shah reported the results of a study in the late 1990s that noted that $11 billion was spent on ice cream in Europe, while American pets consumed $17 billion worth of pet food. At the same time, the cost of providing a basic education for every child in the developing world would cost an additional $6 billion. Nine billion dollars would provide universal water and sanitation facilities and $12 billion would provide reproductive health services to every woman in a developing country.

Progress, but Not for Everyone

Some countries report they have lifted a percentage of their citizens out of poverty. World economists frequently cite China's dramatic success in raising its standard of living. In less than twenty-five years, the percentage of China's population that fell below the poverty line decreased from 64 percent in 1981 to only 4 percent in 2004. Educated people who live and work in China's big cities generally have ample food, comfortable shelter, and ready access to health care. They own cars, computers, cell phones, and other luxuries associated with a comfortable income. However, rural peasants do not fare as well. A *New York Times* article explains: "In village after village, people are too poor to heat their homes in the winter and many lack basic comforts like running water. Mobile phones, a near ubiquitous [almost everywhere] symbol of upward mobility throughout much of this country, are seen as an impossible luxury."[9] Though poverty rates were higher overall in the early 1980s, the lives of most

More than half of the people in the world struggle in poverty each day.

Chinese citizens at that time closely resembled the lives of their neighbors. Now, Chinese society is sharply divided like the societies of many of the wealthiest nations.

While defining poverty may seem like a vocabulary exercise, antipoverty programs use the statistics and definitions of poverty to drive their programs. Governments, politicians, and organizations that battle poverty wield the numbers to suit their purposes. Each change in the definition of poverty, like each change in the poverty line, has repercussions. Likewise, the causes of poverty are also wide ranging and not fully understood. Each cause has multiple effects. Each effect becomes another cause; however, no matter how it is defined or why it is so widespread, one truth cannot be denied: In the first decade of the twenty-first century, over 3 billion people on the earth—more than half of the people in the world—struggle in poverty each day.

UNDERSTANDING
POVERTY'S CAUSES

Poverty, like any affliction, has both symptoms and causes. The symptoms, such as hunger and malnutrition, poor health, lack of education, and poor housing, can be treated. But fighting poverty also involves figuring out why it happens in the first place. Powerful forces determine who is rich, who is poor, and what that means. Some of these forces are natural—the environment, extreme climate, harsh terrain, disease—and many are human-made: wars, corruption, failed economic policies, politics, racial, and gender biases.

Experts, including economists, anthropologists, political scientists, and other social scientists work to better understand the causes of poverty. This understanding is important in the attempt to fight poverty and prevent it from occurring in the future. For example, lack of understanding often causes wealthier people to blame the poor for their own poverty, making governments and the public less inclined to extend a helping hand. If poverty is seen as the result of factors that nations and individuals cannot control, then aid from wealthy nations and individuals is more forthcoming.

Understanding the causes of poverty may also enable those who fight poverty to break the chain of consequences that result once the cycle of poverty is in motion. As the causes are brought to light, the battle to fight poverty and prevent it in the first place can be waged more effectively.

Some Places Have All the Luck

Jared Diamond, a professor of geography and environmental science at the University of California at Los Angeles is one expert who devotes his work to determining why people in some parts of the world thrive while others struggle. In his book *Guns, Germs, and Steel*, Diamond examines ten thousand years of human history and concludes that "geographic luck" is the key to success, countering those who attribute poverty and wealth to innate intelligence, motivation, or creativity.

THE DISEASE OR ITS SYMPTOMS?

"Very often a lack of jobs and money is not the cause of poverty, but the symptom. The cause may lie deeper in our failure to give our fellow citizens a fair chance to develop their own capacities."—Lyndon Johnson, American president, 1963–1969

Lyndon Johnson, State of the Union address, 1964. www.usa-presidents.info/union/lbj-1.html.

Diamond explains that certain wild plants grew in distinct regions in ancient times and were easier to cultivate and more nutritious than others. This led to the development of farming in some places. Plentiful harvests provided time for people to develop other skills. Civilizations with advanced skills gained power and expanded.

Diamond extends his concept of geographic luck from plants to animals. He counts over 2 million species of animals in the world. Nonetheless, only fourteen species of mammals weighing over 100 pounds (45kg) have been successfully domesticated. Domesticated animals provided people with certain advantages, such as meat, milk, fur, skin, and muscle power. Not one in the group of domesticated animals is native to New Guinea, Australia, sub-Saharan Africa, or the entire continent of North America.

While early native civilizations flourished in North America, it was not until the Europeans settled the continent in large numbers that North America became a dominant world power. European settlers brought horses, domesticated cattle, guns, and powerful weapons to North America. In effect, Europeans carried Europe's geographic advantages across the ocean when they settled the continent. Diamond concludes: "History followed different courses for different peoples because of differences among peoples' environments, not because of biological differences among peoples themselves."[10]

Globalization: Cause or Cure?

Diamond's work is filled with evidence of the intelligence, motivation, and creativity of people from cultures that historically struggle. Since civilizations first blossomed, people's resourcefulness has been reflected in how they produced goods and traded with distant cultures. Until recent times, trade was limited to products and crops. These goods, now known as commodities, are manufactured or grown in one physical place and then shipped to another. But trade has expanded. In the beginning of the twenty-first century, trade included services, money, and

The Port of Oakland in California is a perfect example of globalization and how goods are traded between countries.

information, which have no physical roots, in addition to commodities. Everything moves with increasing ease among nations. The network that moves money and information is not a network of freighters, trucks, and trains, but a network powered by the Internet.

The fluid movement of goods, services, and information among countries is called "globalization." One outcome of globalization is the increasing competition between countries for valuable resources, including knowledge and ideas. Countries compete for talented workers; they compete for tourists; they compete to have multinational businesses base headquarters in their cities. Each time one country outdoes another in this ongoing competition, the winner is rewarded in increased income and tax revenues. The losing country faces fewer jobs and increased poverty.

Advocates of globalization insist that it spreads the world's wealth. Critics charge that it hurts the poor. A book titled *Globalization and Poverty* published in 2007 by the National Bureau of Economic Research explores these issues. It concludes that the poor benefit from globalization if they are part of a country's formal economy. They must have credit, the ability to travel to regions that employ workers, and the technical know-how to fulfill requirements of new jobs. But there is also evidence that the poor suffer from globalization.

Most experts agree that globalization is responsible for increasing the inequality among people who live in the same country. New businesses and wealth that pour into metropolitan areas enrich the lives of city dwellers. They bring vitality and purpose. But people who live in rural villages do not reap the same rewards. Their marginal livelihoods are often threatened as new businesses and modern farms prosper, widening the gap between rich and poor.

The complexity of globalization contributes to the difficulty in assessing its effects. In a lecture titled "Globalization and the Fight Against Poverty" Robert I. Lerman, former director of the Urban Institute's Labor and Social Policy Center, explains that, in theory, globalization encourages growth, lowers poverty, and reduces inequality among countries. Lerman acknowledges the difficulty of pinpointing why some previously poor countries in Asia have prospered in response to globalization, while others—especially in Africa and Latin America—continue to struggle.

Lerman also notes that modern media have raised the world's awareness about poverty. He says, "More than ever, people can see or read about swollen stomachs of hungry African children, 11-year-old Asian children working in sweatshops, and Haitian families living in mud huts without medical care, electricity, or clean water. At the same time, many of the richest people are global celebrities."[11] Lerman cautions, however, against confusing growing awareness of poverty with increasing incidence of poverty. Though the media focus more attention on poverty than they once did, this increase in focus does not necessarily reflect accurately how poverty has changed. On the contrary, Lerman points to decreases in poverty in parts of China and India over the past two decades. He credits globalization with progress in those countries.

HUNGRY PEOPLE ARE DESPERATE

"[Too] many developing countries have neglected investment in agriculture, leading to starvation and malnutrition. Hungry people are desperate people, and periodic famines and food shortages can cause mass migrations that disrupt entire regions."—Richard Lugar, U.S. senator from Indiana

U.S. Senate press release, "Lugar Encourages Obama to Focus on Food, Energy, Corruption," July 10, 2009. http://lugar.senate.gov/press/record.cfm?id=315621&&.

Lerman admits the topic of globalization and poverty is complex and multifaceted. But, he concludes, "it is time for opponents and proponents of globalization to join forces to help low-income countries expand their access to rich country markets and develop and nurture their governing institutions so that the world's poor gain from the benefits of a more integrated world."[12]

When Businesses Go Abroad

One outcome of globalization is the movement of American manufacturing centers to cities overseas. Workers in many developing countries are willing to work for less money than American workers. When an American company, such as an automobile manufacturer, moves its factories to a foreign city and hires workers there to make its products, it is said to be *outsourcing* its labor force. Each job that is outsourced involves the loss of a job in the home country and the addition of a job overseas.

Outsourcing has disadvantages beyond the loss of jobs for some people. In the United States and other developed countries that outsource jobs, strict laws govern wages and benefits, manufacturing quality, and the safety of workers. In other parts of the world, however, the pressure to produce goods quickly and cheaply often results in less oversight and the exploitation

At a Michigan rally, people protest to save automobile manufacturing jobs from being outsourced to developing countries.

of workers. Outsourcing can mean substandard working conditions, child labor, low wages, and poor quality.

In March 2009 International Business Machines (IBM), a major American technology company, announced plans to lay off thousands of U.S. workers and outsource the jobs to India. Workers' rights advocates in the United States objected and criticized IBM for this move. Ron Hira, a professor of public policy at the Rochester Institute of Technology and author of the book *Outsourcing America*, explains that IBM is not the only company that is increasing profits by decreasing its American workforce. He notes, "You really do need the American public to sort of stand up and say, 'Wait a second. This is just not right.' . . . I certainly hope that there's a backlash, because there should be. This is bad for America."[13] In fact, poverty in the United States is on the rise, at least partly as a result of unemployment. Unemployment in the United States in 2009 hit levels not seen in the country since the Great Depression in the 1930s.

What is bad for American workers, however, can be good for workers in other countries. Outsourcing creates jobs overseas and helps reduce poverty in developing nations. This significant shift in location of jobs is demonstrated when American customers telephone a company's billing department or product support line and increasingly find themselves connected to a service center in India. Workers there learn to speak English with American accents and adopt American names in order to increase customer satisfaction. They are happy to have the work.

"Energy Poverty" Is Widespread

Many developing countries suffer from "energy poverty," a term used by Robert Freling, executive director of the Solar Electric Light Fund (SELF). SELF delivers solar power and wireless communications to rural villages throughout the world. One out of every four people on the planet lacks regular access to electricity. That means that every night, when the sun goes down, the only light that 1.6 billion people see before sunrise is the light from burning kerosene or wood.

The lack of energy has powerful consequences. According to Freling, "At the village level, energy poverty means you can't pump water regularly, there's no communications, no way to have adult literacy classes, and certainly no way to run computers at school. Energy poverty creeps into every single aspect of existence and wipes out any hope of climbing out of poverty into the twenty-first century."[14] Countries that do not have consistent energy cannot benefit from the lightning-speed communications that they need to contribute to and benefit from the growing interconnectedness of the world's economy. They are left out of the exchange of ideas and resources that take place among countries that are plugged into the global marketplace.

Energy poverty is the result of many factors. In some regions, rapid population growth overwhelms available energy supplies. In others, the high cost of oil and gas limits access to energy. Droughts undermine hydroelectric power plants that require fast-flowing rivers and full dams to operate. Corruption plagues many developing countries, which results in money spent recklessly. Countries plagued by corruption or ongoing civil wars, such as those in parts of Asia and Africa, do not function well enough to manage expensive, complex energy grids.

Corruption Steals from the Poor

Corruption is blamed for more than energy shortages. In fact, corruption is blamed for much of the ongoing poverty in developing countries. Human Rights Watch points to the dictatorship of President Teodoro Obiang Nguema Mbasogo of Equatorial Guinea as a prime example. The dictator mishandled billions of dollars in oil revenue. Since vast fields of oil were discovered there in the 1990s, the country's financial resources surged over 5000 percent. The country is now the fourth-largest oil producer in sub-Saharan Africa. Yet most of Equatorial Guinea's 500,000 people still live in dire poverty. In 2005 the dictator's son spent $43.5 million on a lavish lifestyle, which is more than the government spent the same year on education. Arvind Genesan of Human Rights Watch explains: "Here is a country where people should have the per capita wealth of Spain or Italy, but instead they live in poverty worse than in Afghanistan or Chad. This is a testament to the government's corruption, mismanagement, and callousness toward its own people."[15]

Corruption Contributes to Poverty

Rank	Country/Territory	CPI 2009 Score
1	New Zealand	9.4
2	Denmark	9.3
3	Singapore	9.2
3	Sweden	9.2
5	Switzerland	9.0
6	Finland	8.9
6	Netherlands	8.9
8	Australia	8.7
8	Canada	8.7
8	Iceland	8.7
11	Norway	8.6
12	Hong Kong	8.2
12	Luxembourg	8.2
14	Germany	8.0
14	Ireland	8.0
16	Austria	7.9
17	Japan	7.7
17	United Kingdom	7.7
19	United States	7.5
55	South Africa	4.7
79	China	3.6
89	Mexico	3.3
146	Kenya	2.2
146	Russia	2.2
176	Iraq	1.5
176	Sudan	1.5
178	Myanmar	1.4
179	Afghanistan	1.3
180	Somalia	1.1

Taken from: http://www.transparency.org/policy_research/surveys_indices/cpi/2009/cpi_2009_table.

In 2009 Transparency International's report entitled "Corruption Perception Index" ranked 180 countries from zero (very corrupt) to ten (very clean) and showed that corruption is global and contributes to ongoing poverty.

Widespread Corruption Contributes to Poverty

Corruption is not limited to Africa. A 2008 report by Transparency International (TI), a Canadian human rights group, reported that corruption is global and contributes to ongoing poverty. In a 2009 report titled "Corruption Perceptions Index," TI ranked 180 countries from zero (very corrupt) to ten (very clean). Denmark, New Zealand, Singapore, and Sweden received top scores, while Somalia, Afghanistan, and Myanmar ranked at the bottom. Asked what the wealthy nations could do to help low-income countries combat corruption, TI chairman Huguette Labelle said: "I would like to say, they should start at home. And they should make sure that they do not practice double standards."[16] The United States scored 7.5 and ranked nineteenth. The United Kingdom and Japan each received scores of 7.7.

ECONOMIC GROWTH IS STUNTED BY DISEASE

"You cannot drive economic growth in a place where 50 percent of the people are infected with malaria or half of the kids are malnourished or a third of the mothers are dying of AIDS."
—Thomas L. Friedman, American journalist and author

Thomas L. Friedman, *The World Is Flat*. New York: Farrar, Straus & Giroux, 2005, p. 378.

Labelle sees a direct link between corruption and poverty. She explains: "If you are in a country with a lot of natural resources, with a lot of money moving into the government, but that money is being diverted into fiscal havens instead of going in for the development of a country, that does mean that the school will not be built, the health system will not be there, and the infrastructure will be weak, so that we will have poverty as a result."[17] She points out that wealthy countries are also susceptible to corruption, citing foreign bribery scandals. She believes conditions of aid should include built-in systems that ensure transparency (allowing nothing to be hidden). And donations from foreign countries or organizations should target projects that a country really needs or wants.

Immigration and Poverty

Poverty creates corruption and corruption creates poverty. Immigration acts in the same way. People uproot themselves and move to a new place hoping to escape poverty, only to find their move adds to the misery they hoped to leave behind. They may face an unfamiliar language and new customs, rules that limit job and educational opportunities, and a lack of extended family support.

The reasons for immigration are commonly referred to as "push and pull factors." People are "pulled" from their homelands by the hope of a better job, family ties, or an education. They believe they will find better opportunities in the United States, England, France, Australia, and other developed nations. Other times, people are "pushed" from their homelands by civil wars and desperate poverty.

Reporter Sonia Nazario won a Pulitzer Prize for her book *Enrique's Journey*, an account of the harrowing journey of one teenage boy from Honduras to the United States in search of his mother. Enrique's mother left him in the care of his grandmother when he was five and immigrated to the United States

Polls show that Americans want to crack down on illegal immigration but agricultural businesses still depend on cheap immigrant labor, like the workers pictured here, to make a profit.

to find work. This was the only way she felt she could provide for him, Nazario explains. *Enrique's Journey* is both a terrifying tale of his journey and a critique of U.S. immigration policy. Nazario claims that "politicians have put a lock on the front door while swinging the back door wide open."[18] She explains that while polls show that Americans want to crack down on illegal immigration, businesses such as agriculture, construction, food processing, restaurants, and domestic help agencies depend on cheap immigrant labor to operate at a profit. The result is that illegal immigrants who cross into the United States hoping to escape the poverty in their home countries are often exploited and remain in poverty.

The Heritage Foundation, a conservative public policy research institute, published a report by Robert Rector, Senior Research Fellow in Domestic Policy Studies, that also links poverty in the United States to legal immigration. According to Rector, "While the government continues its massive efforts to reduce poverty, immigration policy in the United States has come to operate in the opposite direction, increasing rather than decreasing poverty."[19] Rector claims that the U.S. immigration system favors kinship ties over skills and education. This results in an influx of immigrants who have family in their new home but lack the skills and education to find a good job.

He points out in an article published in the online edition of *National Review* that one quarter of all poor persons in the United States are now first-generation immigrants or the minor children of those immigrants. He adds that roughly one in ten of the persons counted among the poor by the U.S. Census Bureau are either illegal immigrants or the minor children of illegal immigrants. Rector claims that low levels of education and high levels of poverty will persist in immigrant families for many generations. He suggests that poverty in the United States will decrease only when immigration policies favor educated immigrants.

This attitude toward immigration is one that many people find difficult to reconcile with their own backgrounds. Except for those whose ancestors are native Americans, everyone in the

Fighting Frustration with Books

In the rugged mountains of northern Pakistan, residents of the tiny village of Korphe barely make a living. Greg Mortenson found himself in Korphe in 1993 after a failed attempt to climb K2, one of the world's most treacherous mountains. After watching the children scratch their lessons in the dirt with sticks, he vowed to return there to build a school. Mortenson believes that desperate poverty breeds anger and frustration in Pakistan and Afghanistan. Some schools in these regions are set up by extremist groups that in addition to teaching school subjects such as reading and math, also teach children to distrust and fear Western ideas and values. Mortenson's schools, funded by the Central Asia Institute (CAI) offer an alternative. Mortenson points out that most local schools are not training grounds for terrorists but that the children are vulnerable. He says, "And those kids sit in there for 10 to 12 hours a day. Within one year you can take kids who are full of hope and pride in learning how to read and write and turn them into hardened, U.S.-hating militants. It doesn't take very long, as long as you are feeding and clothing and sheltering those kids." As of 2007, CAI has established 61 schools, educating over 25,000 students, including 14,000 girls. The story of Mortenson's mission to promote peace by building schools is recounted in the book *Three Cups of Tea*, published in 2006.

Quoted in Karin Ronnow, "Journey of Hope," *Bozeman* (MT) *Daily Chronicle,* special series, September/October 2007.

Many conservative Muslim schools separate boys and girls; some even promote feelings of intolerance to the United States.

United States is descended from immigrants. This fuels a conflict about the justice of closing the door to new immigrants to reduce poverty rates. The United States, in particular, takes pride in its heritage as a land of opportunity, where anyone can succeed if he or she is willing to work hard.

The causes of poverty are complex, far reaching, and interconnected. The effort to understand poverty and break its destructive cycle is intense and ongoing. Each time one cause is identified and a strategy devised to counter that cause, poverty arises in a new form with equally devastating consequences. The battle against poverty requires an equally strategic and interconnected plan.

FIGHTING POVERTY

Poverty is destructive. It nurtures disease and deprives people of security. People in extreme poverty live in fear each day of going hungry or falling victim to illnesses they cannot treat. But poverty is more than hunger and disease. It deprives people of dignity and hope. People from many fields of study work to identify and understand the root causes of poverty. But whether or not the causes are fully understood, the battle must be waged.

The battle against poverty is ongoing. It has many fronts. Opinions vary widely about how best to battle poverty and who should bear the costs. Some people believe that wealthy governments should bear responsibility and are willing to pay higher taxes to support that. Others believe that the government should play only a minor role and that private businesses and individuals should take the lead in the fight against poverty. Nongovernmental organizations (NGOs), sometimes called civil societies or grassroots organizations, occupy a place in between. They fight poverty and fund programs for the poor with individual donations and government grants. Just as the causes of poverty are complex, strategies to fight poverty are controversial, many sided, and fraught with debate.

Waging a War on Poverty in the United States

The first half of the 1960s was an eventful era in the United States. In May 1961 the first American blasted into space. Two years later, President John F. Kennedy was assassinated. Following constitutional procedure, the vice president, Lyndon Baines Johnson (LBJ), took the oath of office within hours of Kennedy's death. LBJ inherited the escalating Vietnam War and ongoing

President Lyndon B. Johnson drastically lowered the U.S. poverty rate in the 1960s by expanding the role of the federal government to help the poor.

tension between the Soviet Union and the United States. As he campaigned for election the following year, Johnson launched a vision for America that he called the Great Society. Johnson claimed the Great Society would be a place "where no child will go unfed and no youngster will go unschooled; where every child has a good teacher and every teacher has good pay, and both have good classrooms; where every human being has dignity and every worker has a job."[20]

In order to realize his vision, Johnson committed his new administration to a "war on poverty." To wage this war, he urged Congress to expand the role of the federal government to help the poor. Congress passed bills that raised the minimum wage and set up the Department of Housing and Urban Development to protect tenants and control rents. The government enacted a college loan system for poor students. Medicaid and Medicare helped pay for health care for the poor and elderly. By the time LBJ left office in 1969, the number of social programs in the country had

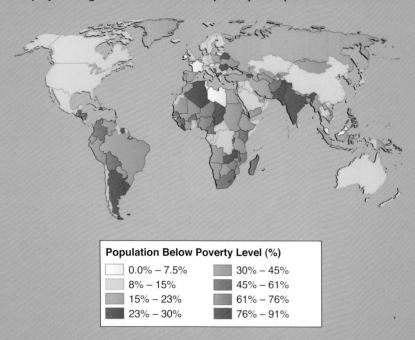

Population Below the Poverty Line

National estimates of the percentage of the population falling below the poverty line are based on surveys of sub-groups, with the results weighted by the number of people in each group. Definitions of poverty vary considerably among nations. For example, rich nations generally employ more generous standards of poverty than poor nations.

Population Below Poverty Level (%)

0.0% – 7.5%	30% – 45%
8% – 15%	45% – 61%
15% – 23%	61% – 76%
23% – 30%	76% – 91%

Taken from: CIA World Factbook, January 1, 2009.

increased from 44 to 435. The poverty rate in the country fell during the Johnson administration from 22 percent to 13 percent.

This newly active role played by the U.S. government also changed expectations. People came to depend on the federal government to ensure adequate health care, housing, education, income, and employment. They accepted Johnson's notion that it was the government's responsibility to provide these services to those unable to do so. Conservative critics, however, believed then and continue to insist that social programs developed and paid for by the government actually harmed the country by draining resources and making the poor dependent on the government instead of helping themselves. They charge that the victor in the war on poverty was poverty itself.

EDUCATING GIRLS AND BOYS IN AFGHANISTAN

"In 2001, only a million Afghan children were enrolled in school, all of them boys. Today, approximately 7 million Afghan children attend school, of which 2.6 million, or roughly a third, are girls."—Dexter Filkins, American journalist

Dexter Filkins, "A School Bus for Shamsia," *New York Times Magazine*, August 23, 2009, p. 44.

Ronald Reagan, a Republican U.S. president elected in 1980, agreed with those critics. He criticized government social programs as temporary solutions for poverty that create more long-term problems. He argued that government programs create an ongoing culture of dependence on government support that ultimately sustains rather than battles poverty. Reagan spoke for many conservative Republicans when he claimed, "There is no question that many well-intentioned Great Society-type programs contributed to family breakups, welfare dependency, and a large increase in births out of wedlock."[21]

Nonetheless, as the twenty-first century proceeds, the war on poverty has become a global battle as people around the world continue to work to alleviate the suffering caused by poverty. Debate centers around which global antipoverty programs are effective and what combination of private and public institutions should bear the financial brunt of battling what has become a global war.

The UN Provides Security for All

The organization that oversees the global battle on poverty is the United Nations. The UN was founded after World War II to provide security to the nations of the world and to keep world peace. The UN has 192 member countries. It functions as command central to coordinate many organizations that promote peace, safeguard the environment, and provide disaster relief and economic assistance to those in need.

The World Bank is one of the organizations that operates under the umbrella of the UN. The World Bank is not a bank in the traditional sense. It is an international institution that provides financial and technical assistance to developing countries. Most of its financial assistance takes the form of low-interest loans. The World Bank consists of 186 member countries. They work together to promote health care, education, agriculture, building

The World Bank provides various forms of assistance to third world countries, such as lunches for this school in Colombia.

of infrastructure, and sound financial management for countries that need support.

The World Bank carries out thousands of projects in every poverty-plagued region of the globe. In 2009 the bank was involved in more than eighteen hundred projects. The World Bank does not operate alone. Donor countries, member countries that have the resources to loan money, provide funds at low interest rates, and the bank partners with governments, communities, and private businesses on projects to help the poor. Currently the World Bank plays a major role in overseeing and monitoring a cooperative global effort known as the Millennium Development Goals (MDGs) to improve the lives of the world's 3 billion people who live in poverty.

Is Any Job Better than No Job?

"It's sometimes said in poor countries that the only thing worse than being exploited in a sweatshop is not being exploited in a sweatshop."—Nicholas D. Kristof, *New York Times* columnist, and Sheryl WuDunn, American journalist, author, and businesswoman

Nicholas D. Kristof and Sheryl WuDunn, "The Women's Crusade," *New York Times Magazine*, August 23, 2009. p. 34.

Millennium Development Goals

In the year 2000, world leaders from 189 countries gathered at UN headquarters in New York under the leadership of UN secretary general Ban Ki-moon and signed the United Nations Millennium Declaration. This historic agreement commits the nations of the world—large and small, rich and poor—to work together to reduce extreme poverty and tackle poverty's basic causes. The agreement includes a time line to reach the goals by 2015. EndPoverty2015, a Web site devoted to the millennium campaign, explains: "For the first time, there is an agreed [upon] global compact in which rich and poor countries recognize that they share the responsibility to end poverty and its root causes.

A War on Poverty

"Unfortunately, many Americans live on the outskirts of hope—some because of their poverty, and some because of their color, and all too many because of both. Our task is to help replace their despair with opportunity. This administration today, here and now, declares unconditional war on poverty in America. I urge this Congress and all Americans to join with me in that effort.

It will not be a short or easy struggle, no single weapon or strategy will suffice, but we shall not rest until that war is won. The richest nation on earth can afford to win it. We cannot afford to lose it. One thousand dollars invested in salvaging an unemployable youth today can return $40,000 or more in his lifetime.

Poverty is a national problem, requiring improved national organization and support. But this attack, to be effective, must also be organized at the state and the local level and must be supported and directed by state and local efforts. For the war against poverty will not be won here in Washington. It must be won in the field, in every private home, in every public office, from the courthouse to the White House."

Lyndon Johnson, State of the Union address, January 8, 1964. www.usa-presidents.info/union/lbj-1.html.

The world has the money, resources and technology to achieve these Goals."[22] There are eight millennium development goals:

1. Eradicate extreme poverty and hunger
2. Universal education
3. Gender equality
4. Child health
5. Maternal health
6. Combat HIV/AIDS
7. Environmental sustainability
8. Global partnership

Each goal is further broken down into smaller targets that are monitored for progress.

A Far-Reaching Goal

The first MDG, to eradicate extreme poverty and hunger, is far reaching. Some parts of the world, notably India and China have

Although China has lowered its poverty rate, 130 million people still live in poverty—like these women and children in Dong Guan.

made great progress toward reaching this goal. India has become a global center of the telecommunications and pharmaceutical industries. Poverty rates in China have also declined markedly. In fact, China accounts for most of the improvement in world poverty figures. Albert Park, a China scholar at the University of Oxford in England, applauds China's success at reducing its poverty level so dramatically—from 85 percent to 27 percent within twenty years—but points out that over 130 million people in China still live in poverty. He warns that millions will be pushed back into poverty by the economic crisis that began in 2008. Park believes that China's best insurance against poverty is investment in health and education, which are valuable in both rural and urban settings.

Progress toward the first MDG has been mixed. Despite some gains, world hunger has increased overall. In a report issued in October 2009, the UN Food and Agriculture Organization claims that one out of six people in the world—over 1 billion people—do not have enough to eat. The report warns, "Unless these trends are reversed, ambitious goals set by the international community to slash the number of hungry people by 2015 will not be met."[23] The report blames rising hunger on a decade of decline in investment in agriculture as well as reduction in foreign aid.

Though many statistics about poverty and hunger reflect grim realities, individual success stories highlight progress made in some regions. Microfinance, the extension of small loans to low-income people to help them launch small businesses, is one effective program. Another success is the development of NERI-CA—New Rice for Africa. This hybrid rice is a cross between African and Asian varieties and is expected to produce up to 200 percent more than traditional crops.

The Goals Are Connected

Though the millennium development goals are presented as individual goals, the reality is that, like gears, each goal drives the others. They cannot be neatly separated. For example, the second MDG, universal education, and the third, gender equality, are closely connected. This is underscored on the Web site of the Global Campaign for Education (GCE), a grassroots movement whose goal is to end the global education crisis. According to the GCE, "No country has ever achieved continuous and rapid economic growth without first having at least 40% of its adults able to read and write."[24] The GCE also points out that a child born to a literate mother is 50 percent more likely to survive past the age of five years. Universal education is also considered crucial in the fight against HIV/AIDS and malaria.

A Global Economic Crisis Presents New Obstacles

The current economic crisis has presented unforeseen obstacles to the ambitious goal of reducing world poverty by 2015 that was set by the Millennium Development project. In a progress report delivered to the United Nations, UN secretary general Ban Ki-moon warned that if poverty continues to grow, the world is at great risk. "We have made important progress in this effort [to meet the millennium development goals] and have many successes on which to build. But we have been moving too slowly to meet our goals. And today, we face a global economic crisis whose full repercussions have yet to be felt. At the very least, it will throw us off course in a number of key areas, particularly in the developing countries. At worst, it could prevent us from keeping our promises, plunging millions more into poverty and posing a risk of social and political unrest. That is an outcome we must avoid at all costs."

Ban Ki-moon, "Forward: Millennium Development Report 2009," United Nations. www.un.org/millennium goals/pdf/MDG%20Report%202009%20ENG.pdf.

The United Nations Children's Fund's (UNICEF) 2007 "State of the World's Children" report also highlights the connections between the goals. According to the report, promoting equality between men and women and empowering women (Goal 3) "will propel all the other goals, from reducing poverty and hunger [Goal 1] to saving children's lives [Goal 4], improving maternal health [Goal 5], ensuring universal education [Goal 2], combating HIV/AIDS [Goal 6], and ensuring environmental sustainability [Goal 7]."[25] Studies confirm that when women and men share equally in making family decisions, more household resources are devoted to children. The empowerment of women within the family leads to stronger communities. Schools improve and literacy rises. The United Nations Population Fund underscores the importance of this millennium goal on its Web site, where it says, "Gender equality is acknowledged as being a key to achieving the other seven goals."[26]

Clean Water Saves Lives

Goal 7 addresses the issue of safe drinking water and sanitation. Though AIDS and malaria claim millions of lives each year, diarrhea is the most deadly disease of all. Five thousand children die each day from the effects of diarrhea. In the United States, clean water comes out of a faucet, but in one-sixth of the world, plumbing is rare. In many countries women and children spend hours each day fetching clean water and carrying it back to their families. According to a study by United Nations University, ensuring safe drinking water and sanitation is the fastest way to eradicate poverty and improve health worldwide. Water is basic to development. Without clean drinking water, people do not stay healthy. Without health, they do not have the physical strength to grow food, go to school, build solid housing and community infrastructure, or maintain jobs. The university issued a statement that claims, "Simply installing toilets where

People in northern Ghana use donkeys and carts to carry barrels of water from a pond. Not having immediate access to clean drinking water is one characteristic of absolute poverty.

needed throughout the world and ensuring safe water supplies would do more to end crippling poverty and improve world health than any other measure."[27]

But Who Pays the Bills?

The eighth millennium development goal, to create a global partnership for development, may be the most controversial goal of all. This goal places responsibility for reducing poverty on every country, rich or poor. Poor countries must ensure that their policies regarding incoming aid from other countries are clear and distributed fairly to those who need it. Rich countries must follow through on their commitments and provide the aid they have promised.

THE MISSION OF THE WORLD BANK

"To fight poverty with passion and professionalism with lasting results. To help people help themselves and their environment by providing resources, sharing knowledge, building capacity and forging partnerships in the public and private sectors."—World Bank Mission Statement

World Bank, "About Us," http://go.worldbank.org/DM4A38OWJ0.

The issue of the world's governments following through on pledges of aid was addressed in June 2009 at the UN General Assembly meeting on the global economic crisis. Prior to the meeting, the UN Millennium Campaign released an analysis of donated aid from the past fifty years showing that donor countries have provided $2 trillion since aid programs began. Yet, in 2008 alone, $18 trillion was spent to bail out banks and other financial institutions in the world's richest countries. Salil Shetty, director of the UN Millennium Campaign, attributes the difference to political will rather than available funds: "The stark contrast between the money dispersed to the world's desperately poor after 49 years of painstaking summits and negotiations and the staggering sums found virtually overnight to bail out the

Sweet Plumpynut Saves Lives

Every year, 5 million children die from malnutrition—one every six seconds. But the Nobel Prize–winning relief group Doctors Without Borders has developed a simple lifesaving food. Called Plumpynut, it is a paste made from peanut butter, powdered milk, and powdered sugar and enriched with vitamins and minerals. It is squeezed out of a tube like toothpaste and does not require refrigeration or water, both largely unavailable in Niger, named the least developed of all developing countries. It is sweet, so even very weak children will eat it. Doctors have been gratified at how quickly children begin to gain weight once they begin their Plumpynut regimen. When the CBS TV newsmagazine *60 Minutes* traveled to West Africa, reporters witnessed thousands of mothers and children lined up for the lifesaving food. Milton Tectonidis, the chief nutritionist for Doctors Without Borders, explains the impact of Plumpynut: "It's a revolution in nutritional affairs. Now we have something. It is like an essential medicine. In three weeks, we can cure a kid that looks like they're half dead. We can cure them just like an antibiotic. It's just, boom! It's a spectacular response."

Quoted in Anderson Cooper, "A Lifesaver Called 'Plumpynut,'" *60 Minutes*, June 22, 2008. www.cbsnews.com/stories/2007/10/19/60minutes/main3386661.shtml?tag=contentMain;contentBody.

The revolutionary Plumpynut snack, developed by Doctors Without Borders, has saved thousands of children from malnourishment.

creators of the global economic crisis makes it impossible for governments to any longer claim that the world can't find the money to help the 50,000 people who are dying of extreme poverty every day."[28] The Millennium Campaign is critical of the many countries that have not fulfilled aid commitments. Two-thirds of the money promised to sub-Saharan Africa by 2010 has yet to be delivered.

Progress Is Slow

The UN issued the "Millenium Development Goals Report" in 2009 to assess progress in meeting the MDGs. The results are mixed. UN secretary general Ban Ki-moon writes: "Fewer people today are dying of AIDS, and many countries are implementing proven strategies to combat malaria and measles, two major killers of children. The world is edging closer to universal primary education, and we are well on our way to meeting the target for safe drinking water."[29] However, he acknowledges that the poor suffer most from the ongoing economic crisis. He says tens of millions of people have been pushed into insecure or unpaid jobs, and the number of people who do not earn enough to rise above the poverty line of $1.25 per day has increased. Ban encourages the global community to redouble its efforts to aid development in the poorest countries. He professes optimism that the goals may still be reached.

Types of Foreign Aid

Foreign aid is central to discussions about reducing world poverty. There are many forms of foreign aid. Aid is usually categorized as development aid or direct aid. Development aid is money provided for long-term improvement of basic institutions, such as agriculture, health care, water delivery, or energy systems. Direct aid focuses on more immediate solutions to particular problems. Direct aid can be project aid, which targets a specific project, such as money to build a school or hospital. Food aid, another form of direct aid, is usually sent to a country following a natural disaster, such as an earthquake or drought. Food aid may be sent to war-torn countries to help feed displaced refugees. Technical assistance entails sending people

Displaced persons from a refugee camp in Uganda receive food aid from the United States. Food aid is just one type of foreign aid used to reduce world poverty.

who have special skills, such as doctors and engineers, to developing countries. Technical assistance might benefit long-term development or short-term projects.

Investment is another form of aid that can benefit long-term development or short-term projects. Groups of investors offer financial assistance to businesses. If the business is successful, the investors share in its profits. Investments in mining and agriculture, for example, are important to economies of many developing countries in Africa.

Another form of income for developing countries, somewhat related to foreign aid, is known as remittance. Remittance is the money sent back to a country by people who have immigrated. They send money they earn back to their home country to help support their families. Though individual remittances may seem minor, remittances to developing countries totaled about $328 billion in 2008.

What Form of Foreign Aid Is Best?

Aid to developing countries is highly controversial for many reasons. Critics claim that development aid is sometimes counterproductive because it cannot sustain itself. They argue that rather than alleviating poverty, development aid promotes poverty by encouraging dependency. Also, development aid from wealthy countries sometimes targets projects that may be inappropriate at the local level. A hydroelectric power project on the Tigris River in Turkey was highly controversial for that reason. The project, begun in 2006, is funded by development aid from an international group led by a Swiss company. The project is supposed to provide electricity and jobs for thousands of people; however, construction of the reservoir flooded many small settlements along the Tigris and displaced eighty thousand Turkish Kurds from their homes.

Many charities and well-intentioned organizations argue that the best aid helps poor people and poor nations tackle their own economic difficulties. Projects that work directly with individuals or small communities are usually funded by NGOs that raise funds from a combination of donations from individuals, businesses, private foundations, and government agencies. NGOs are often based in developing countries and aid from these organizations is aimed directly at the needs of the local poor. Though the projects might be small, they can make enormous differences in the lives of individuals. Send a Cow is one such NGO that works with widows in Africa. The NGO provides women with a cow and the women then sell milk to support their families. Along with income, the women gain self-esteem and a voice in their communities, where they often speak up to promote better health care and education. And better health and education provide the best chance for people to lift themselves out of poverty.

NGOs are divided into categories. Not all NGOs support small projects. Oxfam, for example, is an NGO that helps people develop sustainable agricultural techniques or methods of obtaining clean water. Other NGOs raise awareness about specific causes, such as women's rights or the environment.

When the Cure Makes the Disease Harder to Treat

Direct food aid generates controversy of its own. Critics charge that food donations deepen the hunger crisis rather than improve it. Farmers in the United States and other wealthy nations are paid subsidies, or fees, to produce surplus grain and other crops. This extra food is then shipped to poor countries, where it is donated or sold cheaply to local citizens. Income from these food sales helps fund organizations that battle poverty. But since these surplus foods are so cheap, critics claim that their sale undermines local farmers. They cannot compete with

A construction worker builds a home for a resident in Sri Lanka after the 2004 tsunami. Project aid is funding that supports a specific goal like rebuilding homes, schools, or hospitals following a natural disaster.

the inexpensive donated food from abroad. Many critics of this so-called food dumping argue that it benefits American farmers but harms the security of local farmers; however, others dispute this charge.

In 2007, CARE, one of the world's largest humanitarian organizations turned down $45 million in federal aid to fund its programs because the money was raised by selling subsidized American crops in African countries. CARE claimed that the sale of these products unfairly competed with the crops of African farmers, making it difficult for them to sell their produce; however, the Christian charity World Vision and fourteen other groups criticized CARE's refusal to accept federal aid. They say that food aid keeps money in developing countries, stabilizes prices, and helps fund charitable organizations. They argue that providing inexpensive products to feed the poor is the primary goal of selling subsidized farm products. If shipping and agriculture businesses also profit, those profits are a secondary benefit, not reason to criticize or halt the practice altogether.

Foreign Loans May Promote Poverty

Much of the aid committed by wealthy nations takes the form of loans. Countries that accept loans agree to certain conditions. These conditions might include deadlines for repayment, interest rates, and other terms. Debt repayment places a heavy burden on developing countries. Resources that might pay for health care and education are diverted to loan repayment. Sometimes conditions appear to benefit both the donor country and the recipient, but in reality, these loans increase hardship for struggling people of poor countries. For example, a donor country might anticipate a future grain shortage and require that the recipient promise to sell back its grain at reduced prices. Farmers in the recipient country have no choice but to sell their crops at set prices to their own governments to satisfy that condition.

In India in 2000, 60 million tons of surplus rice and wheat rotted in storage while the government waited for the opportunity to export it to other countries. Moreover, due to the large

The Link Between Poverty and Terrorism: Fact or Fiction?

It is not uncommon to hear or read that terrorists act out of frustration at being excluded from the benefits of wealth; however, evidence suggests that terrorists and their home countries are often not poor. In fact, of the fifty poorest countries in the world, only Afghanistan, Bangladesh, and Yemen have much experience in terrorism. On the individual level, the nineteen hijackers who flew planes into the World Trade Center in New York in 2001 were middle-class, well-educated citizens of Saudi Arabia. Osama bin Laden, the much-feared leader and founder of Al Qaeda, the international Islamic terrorist group, is from one of the wealthiest families in the Middle East. Furthermore, a study of suicide bombers from 1987 to 2002 found that most are relatively well-off and educated. A recent paper by Harvard researcher Efraim Benmelech and his colleague Claude Berrebi of the RAND Corporation points out that the deadliest terrorist activities, such as suicide bombings, are often assigned to the most highly educated and dedicated volunteers. Cait Murphy of *Fortune* concludes, "There are many good reasons to worry about poverty and to take action to alleviate it. But ending terrorism is not one of them."

Cait Murphy, "The Poverty/Terror Myth," *Fortune*, March 13, 2007. http://money.cnn.com/2007/03/13/magazines /fortune/pluggedin_murphy_terror.fortune/index .htm?section=money_email_alerts.

surplus, the Indian government did not buy all the grain its farmers grew. The farmers had no choice but to burn their useless crops in the field. At the same time, to fulfill another loan term, India purchased wheat and rice—the same grains that were rotting and burning—from American agricultural businesses. The result is that India is the largest importer of the same grain it exports.

Some critics, who are suspicious of government aid, claim that the real purpose of foreign aid is to manipulate a recipient country's politics. This was a common view in the 1950s when the United States and the Soviet Union represented the conflict between democracy and communism. Both countries were accused of using foreign aid as a tool to gain political allies. In recent decades, criticism has also been aimed at the International Monetary Fund and the World Bank. Critics believe the primary motive that fuels aid from these organizations is the creation of new markets for products exported by industrialized countries. While people in developing countries may also benefit, critics claim that the well-being of the poor is not the prime motive.

Africa Loses Aid in a Down Economy

Controversy about whether aid hurts or helps developing countries is ongoing; however, there is no doubt that many countries, such as Rwanda, Tanzania, and Mozambique in Africa, are largely aid dependent. As economies falter, wealthy countries in the West scale back on donations that support these economies. In a familiar chain of causes and consequences, less aid results in political instability. Political instability results in loss of income from tourism, an important source of income in some countries. Farmers threatened by ethnic conflict may be afraid to farm. This is particularly true in some African countries that depend on sales of high-end coffee, teas, and tropical flowers.

WOMEN AND GIRLS: AN UNUSED RESOURCE

"In many poor countries, the greatest unexploited resource isn't oil fields or veins of gold; it is the women and girls who aren't educated and never become a major presence in the formal economy."—Nicholas D. Kristof, *New York Times* columnist, and Sheryl WuDunn, American journalist, author, and businesswoman

Nicholas D. Kristof and Sheryl WuDunn, "The Women's Crusade," *New York Times Magazine*, August 23, 2009. p. 34.

Investment in Africa is also shrinking as the economic crisis worsens. The Institute of International Finance, a global association of private banks and insurance companies, predicts that investment in developing countries could shrink by as much

Because of ethnic conflicts in countries like Rwanda, farmers are oftentimes afraid to farm and therefore unable to produce products for sale.

as 80 percent in 2010. Economies in developing countries are also hard-hit by falling remittances. The World Bank predicted that remittances would fall 7.3 percent in 2009, a $24 billion decrease. The countries hardest hit by loss of remittances are mostly in Africa.

Many Small Steps

President Johnson believed that it was possible to defeat poverty. The population of the world has more than doubled since his administration, and poverty shows little sign of abating. To those who struggle against the suffering caused by poverty, the point is not whether the millennium development goals will be met by target year 2015; they may not. A world economic crisis presents unexpected obstacles, and some situations have deteriorated rather than improved. Still, it is clear that people from world leaders to ordinary citizens cannot turn away from the suffering of humanity. Thousands of organizations, private individuals, businesses, and government leaders devote billions of dollars and untold amounts of energy working to improve health care and bring safe water and food to those who need them. That in itself is cause for hope.

CHAPTER 4

POVERTY AND THE ENVIRONMENT

The earth presents the human societies that inhabit it with a variety of challenging environments. Factors such as distance from the equator, elevation, oceans, ice, various forms of vegetation, and unique weather patterns work together to determine the food that is available, distances that must be traveled to find clean water, the prevalence of diseases, and the effort it takes to stay warm. The success of a society—measured by its ability to flourish—is both affected by and depends upon the environment.

In the same way that other elements of society interact in relation to poverty, humans have a mutually dependent relationship with the environment. People depend on the environment, and they also have an impact upon it. When an environment is stressed, the lives of its inhabitants are usually stressed as well. In the best case, humans and their environments maintain a healthy balance, but that balance is easily upset.

In many cases, when the balance between the environment and humans is upset, the poorest inhabitants suffer most because they often depend most directly on natural resources for their livelihoods. And those who are poor are also most vulnerable to the extremes that the environment delivers—the floods, droughts, earthquakes, and storms.

Poverty, Cities, and the Environment

Many cities have a difficult time meeting the energy, water, and waste management needs of their growing populations. As small farming becomes less profitable, people leave rural areas and move to cities. Many seek low-wage jobs. Highly educated people also congregate in cities to work in telecommunications, pharmaceuticals, and manufacturing. Environmental problems created by crowded living result. According to Cities Alliance, a global coalition dedicated to reducing poverty in cities, "The poverty of the urban environment is not a marginal issue: there is a clear and consistent relationship between weak systems of governance, corruption, urban poverty, and a degraded urban environment."[30] In the best cases, careful planning and well-run government agencies can absorb growing populations. Nonetheless, in many developing nations, both are often absent.

Without urban planning, impoverished people set up living space wherever they can find it. They might congregate on land that is unsafe, unstable, or unsavory and that no one else will take. According to Cities Alliance, the land that is settled in this way by the poor is often "sensitive land that should be left undisturbed, along rivers or canals, in protected areas, on marginal

Children in a slum of Port-au-Prince, Haiti, play along a canal that is contaminated with trash and sewage that pose health hazards for humans and the environment.

and dangerous land, and on watersheds needed for supplying water to critical watersheds."[31] Once slums, or areas of substandard housing, are established in these sensitive areas, the cycle of urban poverty and environmental damage begins. Raw, or untreated, sewage is dumped into lakes, rivers, and coastal waters. Children play in these waterways, and families have little access to clean safe water. Cities Alliance estimates that two-thirds of the raw sewage on the planet is left untreated, creating health hazards for humans and the environment alike.

USING FOOD TO POWER CARS WORSENS POVERTY

"As long as we try to combat poverty within a system that is encouraging people to use food to power their cars rather than to drive less, to use more mass transit, or to demand vehicles that get better gas mileage, we are never going to be successful." —Thomas L. Friedman, American author and journalist

Thomas L. Friedman, *Hot, Flat, and Crowded,* New York: Farrar, Straus, & Giroux, 2008, p. 183.

Cities Fight Poverty, Too

The steady rise in urban population does not necessarily spell doom for the planet, though urban growth presents major environmental challenges. In the first decades of the twenty-first century, cities occupy just 2 percent of the surface of the earth, yet city dwellers consume 75 percent of the planet's natural resources. In addition, 80 percent of carbon dioxide emissions originate in towns and cities. While these facts paint the city as the epicenter of environmental destruction, some experts believe that cities may actually hold the key to saving the environment. Achim Steiner, the executive director of the United Nations Environment Programme, frames the situation like this: "It is imperative to view cities as essential allies in the struggle against urban environmental decay and poverty, not as their cause."[32] He points out that urban dwellers generally have higher incomes than those who live in outlying areas. Also, businesses and city dwellers share markets and services, which helps defray costs. Well-run cities generate funds that can be used to help reduce poverty and improve quality of life. However, in order for this to happen, city dwellers must become allies in the quest to improve city life. This entails taking steps to replace slums with safe low-cost housing, improve educational and employment opportunities, and make important services such as transportation accessible to everyone.

A Successful City Takes Planning

The ideal urban scenario entails careful planning. One city that is often featured in discussions about successful planning is Curitiba, a mid-size city in southern Brazil. When Jesse Lerner became that city's mayor in 1971, he immediately began to implement his vision to improve the city. He oversaw development of a high-speed transportation system that used the city's existing buses and roads. In the space of three days, he closed the city's main street to automobile traffic and converted it to a pedestrian thoroughfare. Business owners initially objected but quickly rec-

People walk in the streets of downtown Curitiba, Brazil, where automobiles are no longer permitted. Curitiba's successful planning is due to its mayor, who developed several nontraditional approaches to improving the city.

ognized the advantages of walk-in customers. They were soon asking Lerner to close more streets to automobile traffic.

Over the years, Curitiba developed dozens of innovative programs that address the challenges of city life. Residents who live in the poorest neighborhoods exchange bags of garbage for bus tickets and free groceries. As a result, 70 percent of the city's trash is recycled. Although the ratio of cars to people is higher in Curitiba than in any other city in Brazil, traffic has declined by 30 percent, and air pollution is the lowest in the country. Curitiba manages growth with a strategy that integrates land use, transportation, and the needs of the city's residents for green space.

Deforestation and Poverty

The careful planning in Curitiba is far from typical, however. Many places in the world lack the organization to plan carefully for growth. The disorganization adds to poverty and damages the environment. Haiti, an island country in the Caribbean and one of the poorest countries in the Western Hemisphere, stands out as a country that has devastated its environment in its effort to provide for its population. Eighty percent of Haitians live below the poverty line, and more than half of those cannot afford even basic necessities.

Some people link Haiti's misfortunes directly to the loss of its forests, which have been logged extensively to provide wood for cooking. The loss of its forests leaves the exposed land vulnerable to hurricanes and landslides. In 2004, for example, Hurricane Ivan blew through Haiti leaving thousands dead; many died in landslides that resulted from the combination of vast rains and the loss of tree cover. The same hurricane resulted in fewer than a hundred deaths in nearby Florida. In a familiar cycle, the consequences of being poor create conditions that perpetuate poverty.

Using wood as fuel creates other environmental problems for the poor. The indoor air pollution that results from cooking over wood fires is unhealthy. The World Bank estimates that more than 1.6 million women and children die each year from respiratory illnesses that result from indoor cooking fumes. That

Progress at the Expense of Nature

"For all the material blessings economic progress has provided, for all the disease and destitution avoided, for all the glories that shine in the best of our civilization, the costs to the natural world, the costs to the glories of nature, have been huge and must be counted in the balance as a tragic loss. Half the world's tropical and temperate forests are now gone. The rate of deforestation in the tropics continues at about an acre a second. About half the wetlands and a third of the mangroves are gone. An estimated 90 percent of the large predator fish are gone. Twenty percent of the corals are gone, and another 20 percent severely threatened. Species are disappearing at rates about a thousand times faster than normal."

James Gustave Speth, quoted in Thomas L. Friedman, *Hot, Flat, and Crowded*. New York: Farrar, Straus & Giroux, 2008, p. 46.

One area that has suffered environmental devastation is Indonesia's Sumatra Island.

is close to the number of deaths caused by unsafe drinking water each year.

Deforestation throughout the world causes a wide range of problems for people and the planet. Scientists express concern for the loss of biodiversity as rain forest plants and animals lose their habitat. Deforestation in South America and Africa also threatens the world with climate change. Tropical trees are able to absorb carbon emissions that cause climate change. In fact, according to an article on the ScienceDaily Web site, "Globally, tropical trees in undisturbed forest are absorbing nearly a fifth of the carbon dioxide released by burning fossil fuels."[33]

The hills of Gonaives in Haiti where extensive deforestation has made the area vulnerable to hurricanes and landslides.

A *New York Times* story by Elisabeth Rosenthal titled "In Brazil, Paying Farmers to Let the Trees Stand" describes the massive deforestation that has taken place as Brazilian rain forests are cleared to make room for lucrative crops of soybeans and corn as well as grazing land for cattle. The Brazilian farmers reap only part of the profit. Much of the wealth flows to the multinational companies that export the crops across the globe. American companies such as Cargill and Archer Daniels Midland purchase much of Brazil's soybean crop to feed cows in Europe and China.

A NATURALIST WITH FORESIGHT

"When we try to pick out anything by itself, we find it hitched to everything else in the universe."—John Muir, founder of the Sierra Club

Quoted in Sierra Club, "Who Was John Muir?" John Muir Exhibit. www.sierraclub.org/ JOHN_MUIR_EXHIBIT/.

Landowners in Brazil must weigh the loss of biodiversity and climate change against immediate benefits to themselves and their families. Though they value the environment, they are hard pressed to turn down substantial offers of cash from corporations to buy their land. Yve de Boer, executive secretary of the United Nations Framework on Climate Change, describes the dilemma: "People cut down trees because there is an economic rationale for doing it, and you need to provide them with a financial alternative."[34] Several alternatives have been suggested. One involves a plan for rich companies and countries to pay people to preserve their forestland. Others suggest paying higher prices for soy and beef raised without clear-cutting rain forest.

Rosenthal illustrates the personal dilemma that faces Brazilians in Mato Grosso, the state of Brazil that is considered the global epicenter of deforestation. She describes Pedro Alves Guimarães, a seventy-three-year-old farmer who migrated to the rain forests there in 1964 in search of free land. He built a hut in the forest and raises cattle. Rosenthal explains: "While he regrets the loss of the forest, he has welcomed amenities like the school built a few years ago that his grandchildren attend, or the electricity put in last year that allowed him to buy his first freezer."[35] These are hard choices. They pit immediate benefits to people and their families against environmental damage that may not be revealed for many years.

Is Water a Human Right?

Forests are not the only natural resource at risk. The world's supply of freshwater is also limited. Though it seems as if water is plentiful, less than 3 percent of the world's water is fresh, and much of that is contained in glaciers and polar ice caps. All of the earth's lakes, rivers, marshes, and streams add up to less than 1 percent of the earth's freshwater. Experts foresee that demand for freshwater will exceed supply by 2025. In many of the world's poorest regions, access to freshwater is already limited. For those regions, increased competition for limited supplies could spell disaster.

For some multinational corporations, though, increasing demand for freshwater presents a business opportunity. According to Johan Bastin of the European Bank for Reconstruction and Development, "Water is the last infrastructure frontier for private investors."[36] At one time, the World Bank and the International Monetary Fund (IMF), an organization affiliated with the UN that works to stabilize foreign exchange rates to promote international economic cooperation and trade, helped finance public works projects in developing countries. They supplied the finances, and the projects were controlled locally. When several large dam projects failed, however, the World Bank changed its tactics.

As a condition of aid, it began to require that poor countries allow multinational corporations to control their water and power systems. Corporations have available money and resources, and they promise equal access to the water. They also charge locals for the water that flows through their systems. Proponents argue that the arrangement benefits everyone. The poor have access to water for the first time, and the companies profit. Moreover, everyone benefits from water conservation. The theory is people will not waste water if they have to pay for it. Critics of water privatization, on the other hand, argue that access to clean water—like access to clean air—is a human right. No one should have to pay for it. Water privatization projects have been attempted in many countries. Some are successful, but popular protest has resulted in many failures.

This scenario played out in the town of Cochabamba, Bolivia, high in the Andes Mountains. In 1999, Bolivia auctioned the rights to the Cochabamba water system to satisfy a condition of a loan from the World Bank. There was only one bidder: Bechtel, a large global engineering firm based in San Francisco, California. Bechtel put together a group of investors to manage the project, which entailed constructing infrastructure to provide freshwater to the city. They were given control over the

A man protests in Amsterdam against the Dutch ING Bank's position in the privatization of water in Bolivia. Corporations see an opportunity to make money by providing clean water for a cost to those who do not have access to it.

municipal water network that served the area's industries, agriculture, and residences. Bechtel even controlled the aquifer, the water beneath the surface of the earth. When the project was completed, the company sent out bills for water use. People in the city were stunned when they received their water bills. Many received bills that amounted to one-fourth of their monthly incomes.

The Power of Protest

Low-paid factory workers, sweatshop employees, street vendors, and homeless children converged on the town's central plaza to protest. Students from the University of Cochabamba held banners that denounced the World Bank and its policies. The government tried to quell the protest, but it escalated into full-scale revolt and spread to other parts of the country. An article by William Finnegan titled "Letter from Bolivia: Leasing the

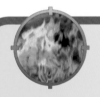

Water: Safe, Fresh, and Hard to Find

"Imagine if, instead of just going to a tap in your the kitchen, or to a water cooler anytime you were thirsty, you had to hoist a heavy vessel onto your head and walk, up to two hours, to a well, where, after filling your vessel—now really heavy—you had to carry it up to two more hours back home. After your trek, how much more time and energy would you … have to farm, cook, take care of your family, especially the sick ones; clean, work to make money outside the home or go to school to get ahead?

This is the dilemma facing hundreds of millions of women and children in Africa, Afghanistan, India and other parts of Asia, Central and South America each day. They live in communities where water is scarce or contaminated or both, and, 9 times out of 10, it is their responsibility to find a safe source, whatever the distance or terrain. They are among the 6,000 who die every 24 hours, because the need for safe drinking water outweighs adequate supply."

Blue Planet Run, "A Startling Reflection on Water." http://blueplanetrun.org/water.

Rain," describes the scene: "The army fired tear gas into the narrow streets of the old city, where protestors had built barricades. Demonstrators blocked all roads into the city; the government cut off power to local radio and television stations. Middle class matrons took wounded protestors into their homes and beauty salons to nurse them."[37] In the end, Bechtel abandoned the water system and left Bolivia. The corporation sued Bolivia for $50 million, but in 2006 withdrew the lawsuit for a token settlement and a statement that it had done no wrong. It is difficult to know who won the Cochabamba Water War, as it came to be known. Foreign investors are reluctant to risk investing in Bolivia, and the country does not have the resources to develop and maintain its own water infrastructure.

Other companies have also run into problems with water privatization projects in Bolivia. Suez, a French company, won a contract in La Paz, Bolivia, when it promised to expand the water network to poor neighborhoods outside the city. One such area is El Alto, home to three-quarters of a million people, mostly poor Indians who have relocated from the Andes Mountains. Finnegan describes the problem: "It seemed that the people in El Alto weren't using enough water. Accustomed to Andean peasant life, they were extremely careful with water, never wasting a drop, even after they had taps installed in their homes. This was good for conservation, but it was bad for Suez's bottom line."[38] The company raised its rates and the general satisfaction with the water project deteriorated. Complaints escalated into a massive demonstration, and in 2005 the government canceled the contract with Suez. An official from the World Bank blamed the failure on thrifty water use by the people of El Alto.

When Luck Runs Out

The water-thrifty habits of Andean peasants underscore the minimum burden that many of the world's poorest people place on natural resources. The poor consume less energy, use less water, occupy less land, and generate less waste. Low-income populations build houses from recycled or discarded materials. They walk or ride bicycles rather than drive cars. And they buy fewer goods, resulting in less factory waste. In fact, the United

Nations estimates that the wealthiest 20 percent of the world's people account for almost 90 percent of the world's consumption of resources. So it seems unjust that when the natural environment unleashes its fury in the form of earthquakes, hurricanes, and floods, the poor suffer most.

There are reasons that natural disasters affect the poor disproportionately. They frequently occupy low-lying land that is prone to floods. Their shelters are generally less secure, which makes them more prone to destruction in earthquakes and landslides. Most people in developing countries do not own insurance to help them rebuild if their homes are destroyed.

Survivors of Hurricane Katrina in New Orleans' Ninth Ward await evacuation after the hurricane. Critics feel that the government did not extend help to this group quickly enough because they were mostly poor and black.

The infamous Hurricane Katrina provides a prime example. In August 2005, Hurricane Katrina struck the Gulf Coast of the United States. The hurricane devastated parts of Louisiana, Mississippi, and Florida. At least eighteen hundred people died. Evacuation of the city of New Orleans, Louisiana, stalled because many people did not have transportation or money to purchase transportation out of the city. State and federal efforts to provide transportation and evacuate the city were poorly organized and inefficient.

The residents of New Orleans most affected by Hurricane Katrina lived mostly in the lower Ninth Ward, a section of the city that is home to a largely poor African American population. At the time, many blamed the Federal Emergency Management Agency (FEMA) for its slow response to the emergency. They claimed that underlying racism was at the core of the issue, since the people who needed help were mostly poor and black. Television networks broadcast images around the world of thousands of people waiting for days in the New Orleans Superdome without food, water, or adequate sanitation. John Mutter, a geophysicist at Columbia University, studies the relationship between global poverty and natural disasters. He contends that disasters such as Hurricane Katrina highlight the social ills of society. Katrina, he says, "was a storm that selected for the poor. Disasters exaggerate social ills. They shine a light on them."[39]

An Earthquake Rattles the World

That vast poverty of one of the poorest nations on earth was illuminated on January 12, 2010, when a magnitude 7.0 earthquake devastated the Caribbean nation of Haiti. The earthquake reduced most of Port-au-Prince, Haiti's capital, to ruins. Two weeks later, people were still being rescued from the rubble, and preliminary reports suggested that over 200,000 people had lost their lives. David Brooks, a *New York Times* columnist, wrote, "This is not a natural-disaster story. This is a poverty story. It's a story about poorly constructed buildings, bad infrastructure, and terrible public services."[40] Brooks reminds readers that twenty-one years earlier, a magnitude 7.0 earthquake struck the San Francisco Bay area in California. While that earthquake also damaged buildings and bridges, only six-ty-three people lost their lives.

The Poor Also Suffer Most from Human Error

Not all environmental disasters result from natural forces. Human error also results in environmental disaster. Often the poor suffer disproportionately from these disasters, too. Their poverty makes them more vulnerable because their livelihoods are less secure. When accidents happen, the poor have fewer financial resources to withstand and recover from hardship.

UNDERDEVELOPED REGIONS GET NO HELP AFTER DISASTERS

"One marker for underdevelopment is the lack of a first response system. When you saw the television reports on the tsunami [in Thailand], you never saw ambulances arriving to help afterward. The main image of 9/11 in New York was that of first responders rushing in to save lives."—John Mutter, geo-physicist, Columbia University

Quoted in Claudia Dreifus, "Earth Science Meets Social Science, *New York Times*, March 14, 2006. www.nytimes.com/2006/03/14/science/14conv.html?_r=1&scp=1&sq=%22e arth+science+meets+social+science%22&st=nyt source?.

That is what happened in Prince William Sound, Alaska, in March 1989, when the supertanker *Exxon Valdez* ran aground. Eleven million gallons of black, crude oil spilled into the sea killing thousands of seabirds, as well as sea otters, harbor seals, killer whales, and billions of salmon and herring eggs. Exxon blamed the ship's captain and spent $3.5 billion in the imme-diate aftermath cleaning up the 1,300 miles (2,080km) of oily shoreline, rehabilitating wildlife, and compensating people who claimed damages. However, a few years later, both the salmon and herring industries collapsed, plunging into poverty thou-sands of fishermen and others whose livelihoods depend on the fishing industry. Exxon denies that the spill resulted in the death of the fish, but many scientists disagree.

Sometimes poverty is the unwitting partner of environmental disaster, adding to the misery and danger of people who are already poor. On December 3, 1984, a tank at a pesticide plant owned by the Union Carbide Corporation exploded in Bhopal, India. At least three thousand people died immediately from inhaling fumes from the toxic gas methyl isocyanate. Thousands

Women walk in the slum next to the Union Carbide factory that exploded in Bhopal, India, in 1984. Poor people set up residences here because it was cheap, despite the hazardous waste in the area.

more died from the after-effects. News reports called the incident the world's worst industrial accident. Yet, shortly after the explosion, poor people converged on the area seeking cheap land, despite the hazardous waste that covered the area. A quarter century later, the area is still a toxic waste dump. An article in the *New York Times* in 2008 describes the scene: "Just beyond the factory wall is a blue-black open pit. Once the repository of chemical sludge from the pesticide plant, it is now a pond where slum children and dogs dive on hot afternoons. Its banks are an open toilet. In the rainy season, it overflows through the slum's muddy alleys."[41] The toxic pond was once sealed with concrete, but the seal collapsed in the intense Indian heat.

The needs of those who live in poverty are urgent. Hunger and disease are immediate. The consequences of ignoring them are dire. The dangers to the environment are urgent, too. Climate change, pollution, and loss of biodiversity occur more slowly, but the dangers they pose are serious. The challenge facing scientists, governments, the United Nations, environmental organizations, and others is to find a way to tackle both the immediate hazards of poverty and the long- and short-term perils to the environment. The goal is to lessen the damage to each without harming the other in the process.

TECHNOLOGICAL SOLUTIONS

With the approach of 2015, the year targeted to meet the millennium development goals, the entire world struggles to cope with many challenges. As a result of the economic crisis that began in 2008, many nations are unable to meet their financial commitments. Diseases still run rampant. Many regions in the world lack sufficient energy to power improvements. Hunger and malnutrition are pervasive. Economists, scientists, and forward-thinking government leaders have begun to consider new and innovative approaches to the entrenched problems associated with poverty.

Bottom-Up vs. Top-Down Solutions

One approach to combating poverty is to search for practical and inexpensive ways to solve the challenges of everyday life. People living in impoverished regions often face challenges meeting basic needs—water must be carried for long distances, food must be preserved, and fuel must be gathered and stored for cooking.

Each year, the Massachusetts Institute of Technology brings people together from around the globe in a month-long International Development Design Summit. The purpose of the summit is to design technological solutions to problems that plague the developing world. Paul Polak, author of *Out of Poverty: What Works When Traditional Approaches Fail?* opened the 2007 conference by addressing attendees, who arrived from more than fifty countries, including Brazil, Ghana, Guatemala, Tanzania,

Although controversial, Congress passed a bill that granted $9 billion to expand broadband Internet service to impoverished areas in 2009. With expanded Internet access, more job seekers—like those pictured here—can find work.

and Tibet. Polak emphasized that solutions must begin not in government offices, universities, or laboratories, but by assessing the real needs of the people facing the problems. Andrew C. Revkin, a *New York Times* reporter, outlined Polak's philosophy: "He laid out the principles of development from the bottom up, including the importance of first listening and watching, then following the old dictum—small is beautiful—with another, equally important one: cheap is beautiful."[42]

Polak emphasized that in order to improve a million lives, technology needs to be simple and mesh with the lifestyles of the people for whom it is designed. He compared the best designs to a drip irrigation system. As a gardener or a farmer cultivates more land, pieces are added to enlarge the system. Thus a good design provides the basis for future innovation and expansion. According to Polak, most technology is not designed to help or serve the poor. Currently, 90 percent of research and development goes to technologies that serve the wealthiest 10 percent of the population.

ONE PHONE SUITS ALL

"Carrying a full-featured cellphone lessens your needs for other things, including a watch, an alarm clock, a camera, video camera, home stereo, television, computer, or for that matter, a newspaper. With the advent of mobile banking, cellphones have begun to replace wallets as well."—Sara Corbett, American journalist

Sara Corbett, "Can the Cellphone Help End Global Poverty?" *New York Times Magazine*, April 13, 2008.

Engineering Is As Old As Humanity

Engineering technology is certainly not new. Technology provided ancient civilizations with the know-how to build the pyramids and devise sophisticated irrigation systems. However, in a world increasingly dependent on access to information, solutions to poverty may not rest in engineering designs at all—even novel and elegant ones. Instead, many experts believe that solutions to poverty will be found in improved access to the information superhighway via the Internet. In fact, Polak credits young people with suggesting some of the most effective solutions. He points out that they are less constrained by traditional ideas. The same technology that most American teenagers rely

Solar Energy Brightens Futures

"Solar energy has not only changed my school life, it has brightened up my future as well. I am sixteen years old and have lived in the rural area for the past fourteen years. In all these past years, I used a candlestick to study and do my homework. The chalkboard has been the mainstay teaching aid at school. When a few solar panels were installed at school in 1996, I did not have even a faintest notion of how it was going to work. A few months later, we received an overhead projector. That was the beginning of a new school experience. The following equipment was later received: twenty computers, two television sets, and a video machine. Recently we have been connected to the Learning Channel Campus and the Internet through the satellite.

Learning is now going to be research oriented. That is, we shall use worksheets and we shall use the Internet as the main source of information. In the past we spent much of our time copying notes from the chalkboard. The school has set itself a new vision for the new millennium. It wants to produce learners who will follow careers in the field of science, technology, engineering, medicine and others. This was a far-fetched dream a few years ago."

Samantha Dlomo, 11th Grade, Myeka Secondary School, Republic of South Africa, winner of International Solar Energy Society Essay Contest, 2000. Quoted in SELF News, "Solar Schools, Brighter Future," Earth Day 2000. www.self.org/news/SolarSchools2.pdf.

Solar panels and wiring provide enough electricity to light schoolhouses and power electrical equipment.

on to network with their friends and play games may hold the key to overcoming persistent poverty.

Expanding the Internet

In late 2008 and early 2009, Barack Obama, then the newly elected president of the United States, worked to persuade Congress to pass a $900 billion program to stimulate the economy as a measure against the escalating worldwide financial crisis. The money was intended to help struggling homeowners and businesses, rescue banks and other financial institutions from bankruptcy, and thereby boost the economy. One percent of the so-called stimulus package—or $9 billion—was set aside to expand broadband Internet service to rural and underserved areas of the country, areas that tend to be the poorest.

Opinions vary widely about the value of this expenditure. *New York Times* reporter David Herszenhorn, in his outline of the controversy, described the advocates' viewpoint: "Proponents say it will create jobs, build crucial infrastructure and expand the information highway to every corner of the land."[43] Furthermore, they claim it will streamline government bureaucracy and make it easier and more efficient to administer public assistance. On the personal level, the Internet will expand market opportunities for small business and provide increased access to online health care and distance learning. The Internet expands the ability of adults to find jobs and improve their literacy. Children in underserved schools will benefit from connection to libraries, news sources, and the wealth of information available to students who are already connected.

Others were skeptical. They compared the project to Alaska's infamous bridge to nowhere. In that case, over $900 million was spent to build a bridge from the small town of Ketchikan on Alaska's mainland to an island with fewer than fifty residents. Some broadband experts referred to Obama's proposal as a $9 billion cyberbridge to nowhere. Craig Settles, an Internet consultant who studies broadband applications in rural and urban areas commented, "If you don't do this well, you end up throwing millions or in this case, potentially billions down a rat hole. You will spend money for things that people don't need or can't use."[44]

Arguments focus on how to expand Internet access and who should benefit from federal tax dollars. Many critics mistrust the motives of powerful wireless communications companies such as Verizon, which stand to receive hundreds of millions of dollars in tax credits. Others believe that requirements that stipulate that everyone have access to new networks deter smaller companies from applying for the funds. These companies are wary about spending limited resources to develop networks that other companies will access at no cost. The details are still unclear, but whatever the outcome, it will take many years to develop the necessary infrastructure to provide the World Wide Web to outlying areas.

The Web Goes Under the Sea

As proponents and critics debate the fine points of the U.S. plan, a new 10,500 mile (17,000km) fiber optic cable opened in 2009 that will provide Internet access to millions of people in southern and eastern Africa. Seacom, a group composed mostly of African investors, financed the submarine cable. It is the first of ten cable connections that will soon link Africa with Europe, Asia, and the Middle East. The Seacom cable provides Internet service that is ten times faster than the current single cable, which has not been updated since 2002. News of the cable was welcomed by many who struggle against poverty, particularly after a 2009 World Bank report directly linked economic growth to improved access to information and communication technology. The new technology will enable businesses in Africa to establish call centers similar to those in India and communicate with businesses and clients overseas.

It could be many years before less expensive broadband connections are available to individuals, however. Étienne Lafougère, general manager for the company that is building the majority of the submarine cables in Africa, explained the delay. He said that access depends on local Internet service providers adding cables to the main system to reach isolated areas. Referring to the information superhighway, Lafougère says, "We are building the highways; then you have to build roads and secondary roads, and that usually takes more time."[45]

Workers pull a fiber optic cable to shore in Mombasa, Kenya, that will provide Internet access to millions of people in southern and eastern Africa.

Which Is Better: Technology or Aid?

The expansion of Internet access in Africa highlights a simmering debate between those who see the solutions to poverty in individual entrepreneurship and those who believe that the solutions to poverty lie in increased aid from wealthy countries. This difference in opinion was evident at a 2007 Technology, Entertainment, and Design (TED) conference held in Tanzania, Africa. The conference attendees included African entrepreneurs, activists, health-care professionals, and artists. Bono, the Irish rock star—an outspoken supporter of African causes—also attended.

Most of the conference speakers reflected the prevailing excitement about the potential of technology to solve the continent's profound economic woes. Andrew Mwenda, a Ugandan journalist and social worker, believes technology offers an alternative to traditional aid. He has been an outspoken critic of traditional aid to Africa and believes that foreign aid only furthers Africa's dependence and passivity. He echoes the sentiments of many when he says, "What man has ever become rich by holding out a begging bowl?"[46] Mwenda points to the $500 billion in international aid to Africa in the past fifty years to underscore his criticism. He claims that foreign aid benefits governments and charities, instead of the sick and poor. Mwenda urged the Africans at the conference to start small businesses, and he called upon Americans there to provide low-interest loans and mortgages directly to African entrepreneurs.

CHOOSING BETWEEN AID AND ENTREPRENEURSHIP

"I think this choice between aid and entrepreneurship is false. If we wait for trade, it will take generations, and people need help now. On the other hand, only entrepreneurship can make us rich."—Herman Chinery-Hesse, founder, Softtribe, a software development company in Ghana

Quoted in Jason Pontin, "What Does Africa Need Most: Technology or Aid?" *New York Times*, June 17, 2007. www.nytimes.com/2007/06/17/business/yourmoney/17stream. html?scp=1&sq=What%20Does%20Africa%20Need%20Most:%20Technology%20 or%20Aid&st=c.

Although the people at the conference trust the power of business and technology to motivate progress, one West African businessman believes that a combination of aid and technology is more realistic. Alieu Conteh, the chairman of Vodacom Congo, spoke about his experience starting the first digital network in Congo. In 1999 Conteh introduced the Congo Wireless Network, with three thousand subscribers. In 2006 he sold the company to Vodacom. Now more than 3 million users subscribe to Vodacom's service. Still, he maintains that it is difficult to run a profitable business in Congo. He claims that the task was more difficult and more expensive than he thought it would be. It has

Growing Up Without Electricity

"My name is Scott and I grew up in Chad, right along the border with Darfur [a war-torn region of Sudan]. We lived in a village without electricity and running water (except when it came running in our yard on the backs of donkeys). We had solar panels—this was in the early '90s—and attached them to a large bank of truck batteries. It would give us several overhead lights, a CD player and other basic electronics for an hour or two a night. That would be more than enough for a community spot. My dad was a doctor and often did surgeries by flashlight when the hospital's generator was not working. The great irony was that the village we lived in had poles and wires ready for electricity, but nobody knew how to fix or operate the big generators provided by foreign governments. I think it is possible to leapfrog like cell phones, as my experience showed. The key is for the industrialized world to recognize this as a priority and a quality of life issue—not simply related to climate change."

Quoted in "Comments to Jeffrey Marlow, Energy Leapfrogging: A View from Togo," Green, Inc. (blog), *New York Times*, August 14, 2009. http://greeninc. blogs.nytimes.com/2009/08/14/energy-leapfrogging-a-view-from-togo/.

taken more than ten years to provide telecommunications to less than 10 percent of the country.

An article by Jason Pontin emphasizes the need for a multi-pronged approach to poverty in Africa: "While the existence of Vodacom Congo may one day help build other businesses, the country's general poverty is not alleviated by the existence of the company. In truth, Africa will need both investment in entrepreneurialism and aid intelligently directed toward education, health, and food."[47]

The Internet Depends on Earthly Power

It may seem as if the Internet operates in a virtual world apart from the earth, but its power is decidedly earthbound. That power can be generated by the wind, by the sun as solar power, or by water as hydroelectric power. Energy is produced from biofuels such as fermented corn and soybeans, and fossil fuels such as coal and oil. The nuclei of atoms are split or forced together to produce nuclear power. Regardless of how power is generated, no one has yet figured out how to bypass power altogether. As journalist Thomas Friedman claims, "Today more than ever, economic growth comes with an on/off switch."[48] Computers need power, too. Computers and the Internet connect people to the world's intellectual resources: the books, libraries, newspapers and news agencies, and people and their ideas. Computers spread information quickly and efficiently, but the World Wide Web cannot be accessed without electricity.

Experts are looking to alternate means to produce energy, such as wind power, for the Internet and computers.

Since energy grids are expensive to develop and operate, experts search for alternative ways to power technology. In some rural areas, old car batteries and makeshift solar panels serve that function. One concept that is currently gaining global attention is known as energy leapfrogging.

Leapfrogging Out of Poverty

Energy leapfrogging takes its name from the childhood game in which children form a line, stoop down with knees bent, and rest their heads on their hands. The child at the back of the line then leaps over each person in front of him or her until he or she reaches the front of the line. He or she stoops down and then the next person at the back of the line continues forward. They continue in this way moving the line steadily forward. Energy leapfrogging, however, is not a game. The fastest way for developing nations or impoverished regions to reach the information superhighway might be to bypass traditional sources of energy and head straight for energy fueled by the sun, wind, or water. Alternative energy accomplishes two objectives. It bypasses the necessity to build expensive and high-maintenance grids, and it safeguards the environment. Both contribute to the overriding goal of reducing the effects of poverty.

Leapfrogging over the Landline

The concept of leapfrogging is also applied to telephone communications. It was not that long ago that making a phone call entailed a connection—not only a cord attached to a telephone but a connection to a complex network of poles and lines. In some places, unused telephone poles and wires signal long-abandoned efforts to bring phone service to rural areas. Cell phones bypass that step. They connect without any lines at all. Moreover, that connection is what many people in remote regions sorely lack and desperately need.

Businesses that stand to profit from cell phones study the ways that cell phones benefit the everyday lives of their users. In a feature story in the *New York Times Magazine* in 2008, reporter Sara Corbett tells of a conversation with a human behavior researcher for Nokia, the world's largest manufacturer of

Telecommunications is very important to people living in poor rural areas, like this man in New Delhi. A phone call to a doctor hours away could save a child's life, or locate the whereabouts of missing family members after a natural disaster.

cell phones. The researcher explains the importance to income and health that the ability to communicate has for people who are poor. Corbett explains: "Having a call back number is having a fixed identity point, which, inside of populations that are constantly on the move—displaced by war, floods, drought, or faltering economies—can be immensely valuable both as a means of keeping in touch with home communities and as a business tool."[49]

Even the very poor invest a high percentage of their earnings on telecommunications. As a family's income grows—from one dollar to four dollars per day, for example—its spending on communication devices increases faster than spending in any other category, including health, education, and housing. People in developing countries spend limited resources on cell phones for different reasons than do people in richer countries. Most people in the United States own cell phones, but they also own landlines, computers, televisions, and cars. They have many ways to communicate. In developing countries, a cell phone may be the sole method available. A mother with a sick child can phone a clinic to find a doctor, rather than walking three hours only to discover that the clinic is closed. Families can check on the whereabouts of other family members, or use the cell phone to take care of errands more efficiently.

Text messaging is also proving useful in developing countries. In some countries, health workers send text messages to remind patients to take medications. In others, people send text messages to ask professional advice anonymously about sensitive subjects such as AIDS, breast cancer, and sexually transmitted diseases. Health experts respond with confidential text messages.

STAY TUNED: MOBILE SOAP OPERAS

"The prospect of marrying low-end mobile phones with the Internet is earning Nairobi [Kenya] notice from outsiders, who wonder whether the city might emerge as a test-bed for tomorrow's technologies. One intriguing possibility is broadcasting local television programs on mobile phones."—G. Pascal Zachary, American journalist, author, and teacher

Quoted in "Inside Nairobi, the Next Palo Alto?" *New York Times*, July 20, 2008. www .nytimes.com/2008/07/20/business/worldbusiness/20ping.html?scp=1&sq=Inside%20 Nairobi,%20the%20Next%20Palo%20Alto?&st=cse.

Cell phones allow many people to become part of the formal economy. The phone functions like a mobile bank. People purchase cash credits through the post office, which are transferred onto their phones. They then use their phones to make payments or withdraw cash. This process was even used by aid organizations after the 2010 earthquake in Haiti. Millions of dollars were donated by cell phone users who texted keywords such as "HAITI" to transfer money from their cell phone accounts to organizations such as the American Red Cross.

It is not even necessary to own a cell phone to benefit from one, according to Polak, who is also the former president of

International Development Enterprises (IDE), an organization that specializes in technology for small farmers in developing countries. In Nepal, IDE set up cooperatives to which local farmers bring their produce. The farmers often seek a cell phone owner to call around to find the best market for their produce. The farmers benefit, and the cell phone owner reaps part of the profit as payment for the service.

Corbett argues that cell phones can be used to promote independence from direct financial aid: "A cell phone in the hands of an Indian fisherman who uses it to grow his business—which presumably gives him more resources to feed, clothe, educate and safeguard his family—represents a way of empowering individuals by encouraging entrepreneurship."[50] Those who promote entrepreneurship prefer this bottom-up approach that is the direct outgrowth of the needs of the people who benefit. The reverse—a top-down approach—depends on filtering money from outside sources, such as foreign governments or charity organizations through a bureaucracy that distributes it. Some of the mobile phone's most enthusiastic proponents are those who question the wisdom of the top-down approach—direct financial aid to poor countries.

More Answers May Lie in the Genes

Freeman Dyson, professor emeritus at the Institute for Advanced Study in Princeton, New Jersey, also searches for ways to apply science and technology in a bottom-up manner. Dyson's devotion to social justice fuels his determination to find ways for science to reduce the ravages of poverty. He claims, "Rural poverty is one of the great evils of the modern world. The lack of jobs and economic opportunities in villages drives millions of people to migrate from villages into overcrowded cities. The continuing migration causes immense social and environmental problems in the major cities of poor countries."[51]

Dyson envisions the day that genetic engineering might stamp out rural poverty altogether. He suggests that once scientists master techniques of genetic engineering, they might manipulate genes to resolve many social problems. They might, for example, use genetic engineering to produce plants with black

Genetic engineering may be the answer to solving certain crises. For instance, crossing different varieties of rice that produce a higher yield could help solve the food crisis.

silicon leaves. These black-leaved plants would convert sunlight into energy with the same efficiency as solar cells, more than ten times as efficiently as plants with green leaves. Not only would this create a new source of energy, it would help alleviate rural poverty. The cultivation of black-leaved crops and forests would be a growth industry ideally suited to rural settings, which would help stem rural migration to the cities. Dyson foresees the ability to manipulate genetics as a source of endless possibilities, most of which reside currently in the sphere of imagination. He envisions trees that produce liquid fuels, for example, and termites that digest rusty metal. He admits these developments seem outlandish, but trusts science to solve society's most perplexing problems.

Dyson's ideas are often considered far-fetched. When his essay "Our Biotech Future" was published in the *New York Review of Books* in 2007, some letter writers disputed his ideas. Wendell Berry, a Kentucky writer, academic, and farmer took issue with Dyson's notion that silicon-leaved plants might help reduce rural poverty. He pointed out that the countryside does not usually benefit when industrial technology sets up shop there. Instead, Berry claims, "industries that are brought in convey the local wealth *out*; otherwise they would not come."[52] Moreover, Berry explains that that the rural poor usually have little control over the results of biotechnology. It is much more common for agribusinesses and biotech companies—not rural farmers—to benefit from new varieties of plants and genes that can be patented.

Sharing the Wealth

Discussions about ending poverty usually focus on ways that the "haves" can help the "have-nots." Well-intentioned experts from many fields wrestle with the complex issues that surround poverty. Programs to alleviate hunger, cure and prevent disease, and educate the poor slowly chip away at the overwhelming problems that afflict people on the planet. Wealthy nations commit money to alleviate poverty. National and international organizations set goals to reduce poverty. In spite of all the effort and all the money, though, billions of people on the planet still struggle to overcome poverty.

Missing in these discussions is the acknowledgment that the "have-nots" have much to offer, too. The world is diverse. The peoples of the world have rich cultures, traditions, and stories that guide their lives. A report by the Linguistic Society of America counts almost seven thousand languages spoken today on the planet. As computers and cell phones sharpen the world's focus, the benefits flow both ways. Robert Freling writes, "Students and teachers become excited as new programs in distance learning are introduced. Electronic friendships are established with people from far-away lands. Music and dance are shared. Cultural diversity is strengthened even as the world becomes smaller."[53] Distance learning connects people. It helps people get to know each other. And when people are connected, they begin to recognize and appreciate their common humanity. In this way, everyone's poverty is diminished.

Introduction: The Cycle of Poverty

1. Quoted in Silvia Aloisi, "UN Warns of Catastrophe as Hungry People Top 1 Billion," *Reuters*, June 12, 2009. www.reuters.com/article/latestCrisis/idUSLC507551.

Chapter 1: Finding the Poverty Line

2. Quoted in Louis Uchitelle, "How to Define Poverty? Let Us Count the Ways," *New York Times*, May 26, 2001. www.nytimes.com/2001/05/26/arts/how-to-define-poverty-let-us-count-the-ways.html?scp=1&sq=How%20to%20Define%20Poverty?%20Let%20Us%20Count%20the%20Ways&st=cse.

3. Quoted in Anup Shah, "Poverty Facts and Statistics," no date, Global Issues. www.globalissues.org.

4. Anup Shah, "Poverty Around the World," Global Issues, November 22, 2008. www.globalissues.org.

5. Quoted in Jared Bernstein, "Economic Opportunity and Poverty in America," Economic Policy Institute, February 26, 2007. www.epi.org/publications/entry/webfeatures_viewpoints_econ_oppty_and_poverty.

6. David Barsamian, "India Together: Interview with Amartya Sen," Alternative Radio, USA. September 2001. www.indiatogether.org/interviews/sen.htm.

7. United Nations Conference on Trade and Development, "Address by Mr. Kofi Annan, Secretary General of the United Nations," February 12, 2000. www.unctad.org/en/docs/ux_tdl365.en.pdf.

8. Larry Elliott and Charlotte Denny, "Top 1% Earn as Much as the Poorest 57%" *Guardian Unlimited* (Manchester, UK),

January 18, 2002. www.guardian.co.uk/Archive/Article/0%
2C4273%2C4337872%2C00.html.

9. Howard French, "Lives of Grinding Poverty, Untouched by
China's Boom," *New York Times*, January 13, 2008. http://
query.nytimes.com/gst/fullpage.html?res=940DE7DD173A
F930A25752C0A96E9C8B63&sec=&spon=&&scp=10&s
q=poverty in china&st=cse.

Chapter 2: Understanding Poverty's Causes

10. Jared Diamond, *Guns, Drums, and Steel*. New York: Norton,
1997, p. 25.

11. Robert I. Lerman, "Globalization and the Fight Against Poverty," The Urban Institute, November 5, 2002. www.urban
.org/publications/410612.html.

12. Lerman, "Globalization and the Fight Against Poverty."

13. Quoted in Mary Snow, Jennifer Rizzo, and Vivienne Foley,
"IBM Draws Criticism for Job Cuts, Outsourcing," CNN
.com, March 26, 2009. www.cnn.com/2009/US/03/26/ibm
.outsourcing.

14. Quoted in Thomas L. Friedman, *Hot, Flat, and Crowded*.
New York: Farrar, Straus & Giroux, p. 159.

15. Quoted in Human Rights Watch, "Account for Oil Wealth,"
July 9, 2009. www.hrw.org/en/news/2009/07/09/equatorial-
guinea-account-oil-wealth.

16. Quoted in Ramesh Jaura, "Corruption Nourishes Poverty,"
InfoSud Human Rights Tribune, September 24, 2008. www.
humanrights-geneva.info/Corruption-nourishes-poverty
,3534.

17. Quoted in Jaura, "Corruption Nourishes Poverty."

18. Sonia Nazario, *Enrique's Journey*. New York: Random House,
2007, p. 259.

19. Robert Rector, "Importing Poverty: Poverty and Immigration
in the United States," Heritage Foundation, October 25, 2006.
www.heritage.org/Research/Immigration/SR9.cfm-101
k-2006-10-25.

Chapter 3: Fighting Poverty

20. Quoted in Digital History, "Did the United States Lose the War on Poverty?" University of Houston. www.digitalhistory .uh.edu/historyonline/con_poverty.cfm.

21. Quoted in Digital History, "Did the United States Lose the War on Poverty?"

22. EndPoverty2015, "What's Different?" www.endpoverty2015 .org/whats-different.

23. Ariel David, "U.N.: World Hunger Has Been Increasing for a Decade,"ABCNews, October 14, 2009. http://abcnews.go .com/International/wireStory?id=8823837.

24. Global Campaign for Education. www.campaignforeduca tion.org/en/about/about-gce/.

25. UNICEF, "Empower Women to Help Children," December 11, 2006. www.unicef.org/media/media_37474.html.

26. UNFPA, "Gender Equality: A Cornerstone of Development." www.unfpa.org/gender/.

27. Quoted in Jon Boyle, "Better Water, Sanitation Keys to Easing Poverty: UN," Reuters, October 19, 2008. www.reuters .com/article/environmentNews/idUSTRE49I2IC20081019.

28. Quoted in EndPoverty2015, "New Analysis Shows That Financial Industry Has Received Almost Ten Times More in Bailout Money in Past Year than Poor Countries Have Received in Aid over Past 49 Years," June 23, 2009. http://end poverty2015.org/files/062309%20Financial%20Crisis%20 Press%20Release_0.pdf.

29. Ban Ki-moon, "Forward: Millennium Development Report 2009," United Nations. www.un.org/millenniumgoals/pdf/ MDG%20Report%202009%20ENG.pdf.

Chapter 4: Poverty and the Environment

30. Cities Alliance, "Poverty of the Urban Environment," 2006. www.citiesalliance.org/doc/annual-reports/2006/poverty_ urb_env.pdf.

31. Cities Alliance, "Poverty of the Urban Environment."

32. Cities Alliance, "Poverty of the Urban Environment."

33. ScienceDaily, "One-Fifth of Fossil Fuel Emissions Absorbed by Threatened Forests," February 19, 2009. www.science-daily.com/releases/2009/02/090218135031.htm.

34. Quoted in Elisabeth Rosenthal, "In Brazil, Paying Farmers to Let the Trees Stand," *New York Times*, August 22, 2009. www.nytimes.com/2009/08/22/science/earth/22degrees .html.

35. Quoted in Rosenthal, "In Brazil, Paying Farmers to Let the Trees Stand."

36. William Finnegan, "Letter from Bolivia: Leasing the Rain," *New Yorker*, April 8, 2002. www.newyorker.com/archive/ 2002/04/08/020408fa_FACT1.

37. Finnegan, "Letter from Bolivia."

38. Finnegan, "Letter from Bolivia."

39. Quoted in Claudia Dreifus, "Earth Science Meets Social Science," *New York Times*, March 14, 2006. www.nytimes .com/2006/03/14/science/14conv.html?_r=1&scp=1&sq= %22earth+science+meets+social+science%22&st=nyt.

40. David Brooks, "At Roots of Disaster: Poverty," *New York Times*, January 15, 2010. www.nytimes.com/2010/01/15/ opinion/15brooks.html.

41. Somini Sengupta, "Decades Later, Toxic Sludge Torments Bhopal," *New York Times*, July 7, 2008. www.nytimes .com/2008/07/07/world/asia/07bhopal.html?page wanted=1The.

Chapter 5: Technological Solutions

42. Quoted in Andrew C. Revkin, "Low Technologies, High Aim," *New York Times*, September 11, 2007. www.nytimes .com/2007/09/11/science/11mit.html?pagewanted=1&ei=5 088&en=35671fa9d3439567&ex=1347163200.

43. David M. Herszenhorn, "Internet Money in Fiscal Plan: Wise or Waste?" *New York Times*, February 3, 2009, p. A1.

44. Herszenhorn, "Internet Money in Fiscal Plan."

45. Quoted in Cat Contiguglia, "New Undersea Cables to Expand Broadband in Africa," *New York Times*, August 9, 2009. www.nytimes.com/2009/08/10/technology/10cable.html.

46. Jason Pontin, "What Does Africa Need Most: Technology or Aid?" *New York Times*, June 17, 2007. www.nytimes.com/2007/06/17/business/yourmoney/17stream.html?scp=.

47. Pontin, "What Does Africa Need Most."

48. Friedman, *Hot, Flat, and Crowded,* p. 158

49. Sara Corbett, "Can the Cellphone Help End Global Poverty?" *New York Times Magazine*, April 13, 2008. www.nytimes.com/2008/04/13/magazine/13anthropology-t.html.

50. Corbett, "Can the Cellphone Help End Global Poverty?"

51. Freeman Dyson, "Our Biotech Future," *New York Review of Books*, September 27, 2007. www.nybooks.com/articles/20612.

52. Dyson, "Our Biotech Future."

53. Robert Freling, "Solar Vision," *International Journal of Humanities and Peace*, 2001, p. 67.

DISCUSSION QUESTIONS

Chapter 1: Finding the Poverty Line

1. Why is it important to develop an agreement about how to define poverty?
2. What are some differences between developing and developed countries?
3. What are some benefits of measuring poverty in absolute terms?
4. Explain why someone who lives in relative poverty may not seem poor to someone else.

Chapter 2: Understanding Poverty's Causes

1. Explain Jared Diamond's concept of "geographic luck."
2. How does outsourcing affect American and foreign workers?
3. The author states that Americans have a "love-hate relationship with immigration." What are the reasons cited for these mixed feelings?

Chapter 3: Fighting Poverty

1. Describe the connections between three of the millennium development goals.
2. According to the author what is the significance of the large gap between money donated to developing countries and money dispensed to bail out American banks in 2008–2009?
3. What is the difference between development aid and direct aid?
4. Describe some ways in which developing countries are affected by the current economic crisis.

Chapter 4: Poverty and the Environment

1. How might cities benefit the environment? Why is Curitiba, Brazil, considered a model city?
2. What are some benefits and costs of clearing the rain forest?
3. What are the arguments for and against water privatization? Explain what happened in Cochabamba, Bolivia.
4. Why do the poor suffer disproportionately from natural disaster?

Chapter 5: Technological Solutions

1. What are some ways that countries in Africa benefit from improved Internet access?
2. Describe the concept known as energy leapfrogging. How is that same idea applied to telephone communications?
3. Explain why some experts believe that cell phones might be the key to ending global poverty.
4. What are some ways that the "haves" benefit from the "have-nots?"

ORGANIZATIONS TO CONTACT

Doctors Without Borders/Médecins sans Frontières
333 Seventh Ave., 2nd Fl.
New York, NY 10001
phone: (212) 679-6800
fax: (212) 679-7016
e-mail: info@doctorswithoutborders.org
Web site: www.msf.org

Doctors Without Borders is an international humanitarian organization that provides aid to people around the world whose lives are threatened by violence, neglect, or natural and human-made disasters.

The Full Belly Project
PO Box 7874
Wilmington, NC 28406
phone: (910) 452-0975
e-mail: info@fullbellyproject.org
Web site: www.fullbellyproject.org

The Full Belly Project is involved with the design and distribution of projects to promote sustainable agriculture in developing countries.

Heifer International
1 World Ave.
Little Rock, AR 72202
phone: (800) 422-0474
e-mail: info@heifer.org
Web site: www.heifer.org

Heifer International works with families and individuals to generate income from the donation of even one cow or a couple of chickens. People donate money for specific projects they wish to support.

The Heritage Foundation
214 Massachusetts Ave. NE
Washington, DC 20002-4999
phone: (202) 546-4400
fax: (202) 546-8328
e-mail: info@heritage.org
Web site: www.heritage.org

The Heritage Foundation is a conservative research foundation that focuses on both national and international issues.

Oxfam International
226 Causeway St., 5th Fl.
Boston, MA 02114
phone: (617) 482-1211; toll-free: (800) 77-OXFAM
fax: (617) 728-2594
e-mail: info@oxfamamerica.org
Web site: www.oxfam.org

Oxfam is a group of nongovernmental organizations from three continents that work to promote human rights and reduce worldwide poverty.

Refugees International
2001 S St. NW, Ste. 700
Washington, DC 20009
phone: (202) 828-0110; toll-free: (800) REFUGEE
fax: (202) 828-0819
e-mail: ri@refintl.org
Web site: www.refintl.org

Refugees International advocates for lifesaving assistance and protection for people who are displaced from their homes by civil war and human rights abuses.

FOR MORE INFORMATION

Books

Greg Mortenson and David Oliver Relin, *Three Cups of Tea*. New York: Penguin, 2006. The gripping story of Greg Mortenson's mission to bring schools to isolated regions of Pakistan and Afghanistan and his founding of the Central Asia Institute.

Sonia Nazario, *Enrique's Journey*. New York: Random House, 2006. The story of a boy's dangerous journey from Honduras to the United States to find his mother, an experience that gives voice to the desperation of poor people in Latin America who risk their lives and the lives of their children in an attempt to climb out of poverty.

Rae Simons, *AIDS & Poverty*. Exton, PA: AlphaHouse, 2008. Explores the prevalence of AIDS among people in high-poverty regions. More than 60 percent of AIDS victims live in sub-Saharan Africa, but the disease is also found in China, Haiti, the United States, and other parts of the world.

D. Mark Smith, *Just One Planet: Poverty, Justice and Climate Change*. Warwickshire, UK: Intermediate Technology, 2006. Identifies the link between climate change and poverty; makes clear that the nearly 3 billion people who live on less than two dollars per day are most vulnerable to change in patterns of rainfall, river flow, flooding, and drought.

Viqi Wagner (ed.), *Poverty: Opposing Viewpoints*. Detroit: Greenhaven, 2008. Presents perspectives of experts in fields related to issues of poverty. Edited for young adult readers.

Sylvia Whitman, *World Poverty*. New York: Facts On File, 2008. Explores the definition, measurement, and causes of poverty. Investigates strategies that the United States, India, Syria,

Democratic Republic of Congo, Guatemala, Ukraine, and other countries are taking to battle poverty.

Web Sites

Cooper Hewitt Design Museum, Design for the Other 90% (http://other90.cooperhewitt.org). This exhibition is based on the premise that 90 percent of the world's people have little or no access to products and services that the wealthier people take for granted. The site displays the work of designers, engineers, architects, social entrepreneurs, and others that improves access to life's necessities as well as income-generating opportunities. It includes links to video demonstrations.

FreeRice.com (www.freerice.com). FreeRice is a nonprofit Web site run by the United Nations World Food Programme and the Berkman Center for Internet & Society at Harvard University. The site offers visitors multiple-choice quizzes in a variety of subject areas and levels of difficulty. Each correct answer results in the donation of ten grains of rice to hungry people.

Globalization 101 (www.globalization101.org). A Web site to help students understand the many controversies surrounding globalization. It poses the question: Is globalization a force for economic growth and democratic freedom or a force for environmental devastation, exploitation of the developing world, and suppression of human rights?

Guns, Germs and Steel (www.pbs.org/gunsgermssteel). The Web site includes a link to the entire television series that was devoted to the work of Jared Diamond, author of the book *Guns, Germs and Steel*. It explores his thesis that "geographic luck" played a major role in human history. Transcripts and supplementary materials are also available.

Heifer International (www.heifer.org). This Web site explains the work that this nonprofit performs in developing countries. A click of the mouse introduces the visitor to the people whose lives have been touched and the projects that have changed their lives.

UNICEF: Unite for Children (www.uniteforchildren.org). The multimedia link on this Web site connects to videos, podcasts, and photo essays that highlight the toll of HIV/AIDS and other problems experienced by children in the developing world.

UNICEF: Voices of Youth (www.unicef.org/voy/explore/sowc/explore_4160.html). The purpose of this Web site is to educate young people and provide them a place to join in discussions, contribute ideas, and become educated about issues relating to poverty. Each year it sponsors a contest for young people. In 2009 the contest entailed writing a radio drama. It has dozens of links.

Podcast

ChicagoPublicRadio,"EradicatingGlobalPovertywithCellPhones" (www.chicagopublicradio.org/content.aspx?audioID=10 310). A discussion of the expanding use of cell phones in developing countries. Includes an interview and discussion with Nicholas Sullivan, who writes about technology and entrepreneurship. He is author of the book *You Can Hear Me Now: How Microloans and Cell Phones are Connecting the World's Poor to the Global Economy.*

Video

Watch the winner of UNICEF's 2007 one-minute video "Make a Difference" contest titled "Bebe—más allá de la niñez." The video competition was open to anyone under twenty-five years old in honor of the fifth anniversary of the UN Special Session on Children. There were one hundred entries from around the world. The winner was produced in Argentina. http://vids.myspace.com/index.cfm?fuseaction=vids.individual &VideoID=11237913.

INDEX

PICTURE CREDITS

ABOUT THE AUTHOR

This is Tina Kafka's sixth book for Gale/Cengage Learning. As always, she enjoys teaching and discovering answers to the world's many mysteries.